# Beyond the Horizon

# WALTER MERCADO

# BEYOND THE HORIZON

## Visions of the New Millennium

WARNER BOOKS

A Time Warner Company

Warner Books, Inc., 1271 Avenue of the Americas, New York, NY 10020

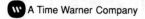 A Time Warner Company

Printed in the United States of America
First Printing: June 1997
10 9 8 7 6 5 4 3 2 1

Library of Congress Cataloging-in-Publication Data

Mercado, Walter.
    Beyond the horizon : visions of the new millennium / Walter Mercado
        p.    cm.
    ISBN 0-446-52066-7
    1. Predictive astrology.  2. Twenty-first century—Forecasts.
I. Title
BF1720.5.M47 1997
133.3—DC20                                          96-42027
                                                      CIP

A K&N BOOKWORKS BOOK
DESIGNED BY PATRICE SHERIDAN

With sincere gratitude I wish to dedicate this book to Carlos Harrison, who has been the alchemist, the magician, and the helper in its creation.

To all my family and disciples, who are my love and inspiration.

To my angels during many lives: Aida y José María, Aida Victoria (Cuca), Henry, Betty, Karmen, Charo, Ivonne, Dannette, Bibi, Henrito, Aidita, Vivian, Miquel, Michelle, Beba, Héctor, Christian, Alejandro, Jeshua, Laura María, and Michael Christopher.

To my wonderful staff: Willie, Vivian, Wilma, Melva, Mabel, Roberto, Alberto, and Vicky.

To my Aquarian Age Brothers and Sisters: Bill Bakula, Jamie Shoop, and Jorge and Laura Concepción.

And to my beautiful people at Warner Books: Diane Stockwell, Joann Davis, and Maureen Egen.

Om Sri Ganeshaya Nama     Om Kali     Om Kali

# Contents

# Beyond the Horizon

# 1

# Beyond the Horizon

The awakening has begun.

Forces dormant for nearly twenty-five thousand years are stirring, swirling throughout the universe, affecting everything and everyone in it.

The very fact that you are reading these words means that you already know or have at least sensed the change in the air, for there are no accidents. You reached for this book for a reason. You are reading these words for a reason. The change has begun.

You might have glimpsed it in that moment of twilight as you drifted off to sleep, when things seemed so clear, so lucid; in that moment when the thoughts that were hard to put into words sprang into your consciousness and you knew—*something*.

It may have come on the wisps of an already fading dream as you came awake, the time when, before you could grab hold of it, the thought that filled you disappeared, leaving only a feeling.

It may have happened at that moment when you read the latest headline in the daily news or saw the latest report on the television, and you asked yourself, "What is happening? What is wrong with the world?" In that moment of insight, you caught a glimpse of the death of the old age and the dawning of the new.

This is the changing of times, the eve of a new millennium, the verge of a new era for humankind. It is a new beginning, a time of transformation, and of a sweeping, collective change among all people.

It is the birth of an age of peace, a New Age, which will lead us to look inside ourselves, then force us to go beyond what we have known. As with any birth, it will be a time of challenge, a time of pain, a time of realization, and a time of ecstasy.

The evidence of the change is all around us. What people speak of as the Apocalypse is already here. We are living it. We are living the climactic moments of humanity. Everything that was prophesied of horror, death, destruction, and brother against brother is happening. Look at Bosnia, for example, and the war horrors there.

But this time should not be looked upon as tragic. Indeed, we are passing through a portal in time, into a golden era of peace and enlightenment. Those terrible events that fill the headlines are the paroxysms, the death throes of an era that is ending. In the closing years of this millennium and the dawning of the new, those paroxysms will turn into cataclysms. The very Earth itself will be rended by the savage grip of celestial forces more powerful than it has felt in nearly thirteen thousand years. But the time of trouble is brief, and once we emerge in the new era, once we have stepped through the portal, the pain will be behind us, disappearing into the past just as the darkness of night disappears with the dawning Sun.

Do not read this book if you are not ready to change your life forever. Read no further if you do not wish to prepare yourself for the New Age, for a whole transformation of humankind and the planet we live on.

The spiritual awakening already has begun—a questioning, a yearning. It stirs in the souls of men and women in distant lands, all independent of one another, all drawn toward a common goal. They may not even be aware of it but, with each passing day, more and more are drawn to it. At first, it may seem a dim, distant light in a heavy haze, drawing glances from people who didn't even know they were searching for anything or that anything was missing in their lives. But once glimpsed, it is compelling, drawing all—the true seekers, the curious, and the ones who have wandered with a tiny sense of doubt in their daily lives. And all, no matter how far they travel in the journey toward that new knowledge of the universe and themselves, will be changed forever.

The words on these pages will serve as a guide to an era of unity, as an instruction manual to the time of peace, as a survival manual for the time of transition, and as preparation for the process of transformation affecting us all. Humanity's supreme moment is upon us, but it comes in a most painful cosmic birth. All birth comes with pain and now nature itself is in labor. The whole world is in labor.

Society is sick, seeking to heal. But healing comes with a change in all aspects—not just in our persons, but in our structures. The healing of the planet, of our Mother Earth, begins by joining in with the transformation that is coming, by restructuring our political institutions, our courts, our laws, and all that has been invalidated, corrupted, and misused. The codes, the texts, the laws, the sacred words—all are crushed, cast aside, eliminated, or written anew in keeping with the new way of the Aquarian Age.

We must be ready and willing for an immense change in the divine order, a change that we are marching toward at ever-increasing speeds. The winds of change are already blowing, but the pace is accelerating. We are nearing the end of one millennium and about to become witness to the new. It is the closing of the time of false hierarchies, of myths that imprison us. We have lived on myths and thrived on false idols. Now is the time for the great awakening, when our questions will lead us to true knowledge. It is time to go beyond the simple beliefs in what we have been told and taught to reach our own wisdom.

It has already begun.

The divinity above, by whatever name we call our God, has set the process in motion. Already, the beings who raise our consciousness, who guide us to the world of tomorrow, walk among us. Already, the cosmic consciousness is stirring in each of us, even in those who feel unease with the change and wish to cling to the past, those who will resist the change.

The New Age doesn't have to frighten us even though it is the nature of people to fear change, especially a change as profound as that which is upon us. All change brings panic and insecurity, for humans are the children of panic. From the time that we are little, we are programmed to fear, to be insecure, to panic. Constantly, we hear the news: California will be devastated by an earthquake; the United States will sink into the sea; New York will be swallowed by the ocean. We are bombarded with negativity. But now is the time for all of us to recognize our immortality, to let go of our fear and embrace life. We must accept life, accept the New Millennium with a divine and glorious "Yes!" Let the transformation come. It is an affirmation that comes not from the mind but from the heart. Aquarius is an era of love, of peace, of knowledge, and of spiritual discovery. Those who do not accept this transformation will not evolve. This is the time for us to recognize our immortality, our enormous divinity. And once we have, we no longer need to be afraid of anything or anyone.

The Earth has been corrupted, on its face and in the hearts of its people. We have been sleepwalking, beating our heads against the wall, not knowing what is to come and fearing it nonetheless. Now is the time for us to fortify ourselves and think of what is in the divine mind, to know that we shall survive even the most negative if we fortify ourselves.

The Chinese have a saying: "May you live in interesting times." We do. The supreme moment of humanity approaches. It is the supreme rebirth, the supreme *renaissance* of the universe and ourselves. But like any birth, it will be painful. The chaos you see around you—the inexplicable horrors of humanity against humanity, the senseless crimes and meaningless wars—are all part of the pain of this great cosmic rebirth. It is the dying spirit of Pisces raging against the New Age being born. We won't just wake up one morning giving each other little kisses and loving one another, black and white, ugly and beautiful. The birth of the new era is not a birth that will suddenly strike us, so that we suddenly say, "Oh, it's the Age of Aquarius. Time to break down all borders, tear up our passports and visas, live as one people, and love one another." It is an integration, little by little.

As we pass through the eras of the universe, we feel the influences like the swinging of a pendulum. This phase has been one of materialism, of looking outside ourselves for satisfaction, pleasure, growth, enlightenment. This has been the era of the "American dream," and the countries that did not fight for that material dream, such as India, sank into poverty. America exaggerated materialism and lost its spiritual values. Now the pendulum swings in the opposite direction, and we will look inside ourselves for these things and more. Aquarius brings with it a compelling desire for spiritual rebirth, but instead of looking constantly outside of ourselves, we will look within to find that we are all linked to the universe and to God.

Already, in this day, people think and dream of a world in harmony, a world at peace. They no longer want to be tied up, they don't want barriers or chains. The age of slavery, the Age of Pisces, is finished. People now seek the unification of all peoples, and we concern ourselves more with humanity in general than with ourselves; in concerning ourselves with all, we care for everyone. We seek ideals, and not the limitations of personal sacrifice. We are souls in search of freedom, feeling as though we are only lent to this world, gaining vision, before moving on to other worlds.

Many have tried to reach back to the ancient mysteries, hoping to find the way to the future. They have taken to holding crystals, to seeking past lives, to chromotherapy and music therapy. This is a resurgence of the old, seeking the ways of the shamans to guide us in a world gone awry. As we approach the new era, there will be an explosion of the ancient wisdoms and we will utilize them in daily life. We will find the ways of the ancient mystics, of the people who lived close to the Earth, close to nature, and realize that we *know*. In the Age of Aquarius, there are no mysteries, there is nothing occult. There are no secrets meant to keep us in darkness. All knowledge and wisdom open before us and we will see what the ancients saw when they looked to the clouds or the trees or the rivers. We will learn from the ways of the animals and from the stars. Everything will be open to us. The Aquarian Age is the age of human enlightenment, of a total explosion of the human consciousness. We step finally and firmly from the darkness, away from idolatry, bigotry, tunnel vision. This New Age that is sweeping in upon us brings the era of light, of peace, of humanity, of unity. It is also the era of technology and space exploration, of discovery and independence. If you tap the resources, you'll find an explosion of creativity.

Would that it were a change that could be marked by a single moment in time, a single, specific date. But it is not. We can mark the exact time at which planets cross from one sign to the next, the moments of their conjunctions and their oppositions. We can mark the rhythmic movement of the constellations in what is known as their natural precession, so that astronomers and astrologers alike can record their march across the heavens.

The stars step at an eternally steady pace. But the changing from one age to another, from the time we know to the time of the future, comes like a gathering rain shower, the change of seasons, or what it is—the dawning of a new day.

Before the rain, the clouds gather, turning darker and darker gray. The wind picks up. Then the first drops begin to fall. All this, before the actual shower.

Think of the changing of the seasons, the changing of the year. As we go from summer solstice to winter solstice, which lie at opposite ends of the Earth's transit around the Sun, we pass through fall. The long, hot days of summer give way slowly and the leaves begin to turn. The days grow shorter. The first cool fronts drift in, lowering the heat. One day may even be cold, but, in the beginning of the season before the cold sets in for good, the warm returns. At the outset the cold comes for a day or two here or there, but, eventually, with every passing day, the cold grows more bitter. It stays longer. The leaves fall. Gradually, ever so gradually, the night grows longer than the day, taking over by mere minutes every day, so that we hardly notice. Then, the first snow falls, though it may just as quickly be melted off by the still powerful Sun. Still, one day, in the coldest climes at least, the snow comes and stays—until once again, as the Earth continues its arc around the Sun, the days begin to grow longer, warmer.

Get up early enough and you will see the lightening of the sky. The black of night gives way slowly to a lighter shade of gray. Then on the horizon, the first streaks of red and orange pierce the night, signaling the rising Sun. In moments, it seems, the bright light of morning bursts forth to reign through the long of the day.

For a while—whether we speak of a day, a season, or an astrological age—what was and what will be overlap, crossing from the dominant influence of one to the dominant influence of the other. Between night and day is twilight; between summer solstice and winter solstice is fall. And just as in the Bible it says "to every season," so too for the seasons of cosmic influence, for the ages of Earth, and for us who live on it.

But summer and winter are opposites, as are night and day, while the changing of the ages of the Earth are like the ticking of a great cosmic clock, in which each hour is distinctly and vastly different from the one just past and the one about to come. In the long time from the birth of the universe to the present, the Earth has ticked through many ages. But because we each have such a limited time in this life, none of us has or will live to see a full age; we have but a few minutes in any one of the universe's great hours.

Still, those minutes are enough to allow us to see the full glory and impact of the coming New Age, the Age of Aquarius, because we stand precisely in the final moments of twilight, between the fading of the old and the dawning of the new.

On January 12, 1996, Uranus, the planet of revolution and reform, returned to its celestial throne, Aquarius. That, just two months after Pluto, the great destroyer, slipped into Sagittarius, the sign of expansion, so that its influence would be magnified. It could mean only one thing: the time had come for the destruction of the old, of the ways and thinking of the past, to open the way to rebuild with the new.

A mere two days after Uranus made its triumphant reentry into Aquarius, the walls of racism cracked in the tiny Central American country of Guatemala, where, for the first time in that nation's history, a native Maya was elected mayor of a major city with real power. A hundred years before, Mayan mayors held seats alongside Ladino mayors of mixed Spanish and Native American ancestry. But the Mayan officials were named merely to keep Mayan workers, who were little more than slaves, in check. What happened then at the start of 1996, the election of a Mayan mayor to truly take charge of a major city, was, in Guatemala, as significant as any breakthrough of the civil rights movement in the United States and equally significant as a sign that the Age of Aquarius was, in fact, dawning. It was a historic moment because racism had become so ingrained in parts of Guatemala that in many ways it was compared to the South African policy of racial separation known as apartheid. Just twelve years earlier, a candidate from the same movement appeared to have won the post, but he was blocked from taking power by the army and, eventually, assassinated. This time, in keeping with the spirit of the New Age, the change came peacefully in a legal, open, and free election.

But the influence of Aquarius did not wait for Uranus to return to it. Like the first graying of the morning sky as night gives way to dawn, the first glimpses of the influence of Aquarius reach back nearly a hundred years to the Industrial Revolution. Aquarius loves technology, and it is no surprise that the shift from the Age of Pisces to that of Aquarius would give rise to assembly lines and great factories, to the shift from an agricultural society to an industrial one. But another dominant characteristic of Aquarius is humanity, and, therefore, it is even less of a surprise that the increasing influence of Aquarius would give rise to the birth of workers' unions and communism, or at least to their originally stated principles. Communism was supposed to be a collective effort, an experiment in communal living in which all would share the benefits "from each according to his abilities, to each according to his needs," as Karl Marx wrote. The birth of the Soviet Union then is clearly an Aquarian event in its conception, despite what it became under the influence of greedy and ruthless leaders.

Its collapse may be even more Aquarian.

Whatever its true intention at the outset, the Communist experiment turned sour, its rulers still under the sway of Pisces, seeking to dominate and control. The Soviet Union became a symbol of oppression over its people. Dissidents were executed or locked in horrible gulags, prisons of the most deplorable kind in the most bitter of environments: Siberia. The bricks and barbed wire of the Berlin Wall stood in mute testimony of the repression, an "iron curtain," as it was termed, lined with armed guards ready to shoot any who tried to escape. Then suddenly, or so it seemed, the Soviet Union came crashing down, iron curtain and all. Credit it to the Aquarian trait of independence, complete with evidence that the Aquarian Age will bring with it a golden era of freedom for all humanity.

The fall of the Soviet Union began with rebelling republics rallying for independence, along with the subjects of Soviet satellites. The independence movement swept across Eastern Europe like a wildfire whipped up by the wind. And on November 9, 1989, the Berlin Wall itself, the very symbol of the repression, came tumbling down, torn apart by East Berliners swinging hammers. Not a shot was fired. The following year, Berlin, divided since World War II, was reunited.

Then, on a rainy Moscow day in the summer of 1991, a group of dissatisfied Communist hard-liners sent out their armies to seize control of the government. Dissatisfied with the direction toward openness taken by Mikhail Gorbachev, the generals decided to stage a coup and take command. Gorbachev had set the nation on an almost breathless race toward reform in the previous three years, and the generals claimed the country was on the brink of crisis. Gorbachev was locked in the dacha where he was vacationing outside the capital city and tanks rolled in front of the Kremlin. But in a crowning example of the influence of Aquarius, thousands of outraged Muscovites massed to face the guns, and the soldiers would not fire. It was a passive showdown that turned into a peaceful revolution. A mere sixty-three hours after it began, the standoff finished and the coup collapsed. As it ended, the tanks still stationed in Red Square, a band named Dirty Metal played once-prohibited rock music along the banks of the Moscow River in a scene that one reporter described as a "Russian Woodstock." To shouts of "Russia is free," the coup collapsed, and by December, the Soviet Union itself followed.

Václav Havel, the Czech writer whose work was banned for denouncing the Soviet invasion of Czechoslovakia in 1968 but who went on to inspire the public protests that brought the end of Communist rule there, was elected president of his homeland in 1989. He, too, hinted that he had seen the dawning New Age as he accepted the Philadelphia Liberty Medal in 1994. On that occasion he said, "It is as if something were crumbling, decaying, and exhausting itself, while something else, still indistinct, were arising from the rubble."

The collapse of the Soviet bloc is not the only sign of the growing influence of Aquarius. It showed itself again in the Middle East, which seemed doomed to be forever bathed in the blood of warring Palestinians and Jews. Hardly a day went by without a report of a car bombing or a terrorist attack. Israeli Prime Minister Yitzhak Rabin and PLO Chairman Yasir Arafat were avowed enemies, seemingly without even the faintest hope of rapprochement. Peace efforts initiated by outsiders failed again and again, and the violence raged on, the death toll continuing to rise. Then, in what many thought was yet another ill-fated attempt at reconciliation, yet another futile series of meetings, the United States brought the enemies together to talk. On a brilliant September day in 1993, the lifelong enemies, Rabin and Arafat, flanked the U.S. president on the lawn of the White House and shook hands. This, just two short years after Arafat had supported Iraq's missile attacks on Israel during the Persian Gulf War.

In the words of Rabin, the time had come for even enemies to put aside the past, to lay down their arms, to think of the future, and to end the violence. It was time, he said, to wage "the most difficult battle of our lives—the battle for peace."

Two years later, as the former enemies met once again in Washington to sign the Israeli-Palestinian Interim Agreement, Rabin declared, "Here we stand before you—men whose fate and history have sent on a mission of peace—to end once and for all one hundred years of bloodshed. Peace has no borders."

It was a peace marred by more violence, a peace most thought would fail, a peace that would give rise to tragic rage within Israel itself—rage that would claim the life of Rabin when he was assassinated by a member of a right-wing fringe group just months after speaking those words. But even with his death the peace would not die. The peace seemed fortified by the outrage over the assassination, with leaders the world over vowing to make it permanent, determined, at least, to make the very Aquarian effort of uniting for humanity.

The Aquarian influence showed itself also in South Africa, where an oppressed multitude that far outnumbered their rulers finally won their hard-earned place in the political domain of that country. It showed itself in the United States a quarter of a century earlier, with the civil rights movement, when African Americans rose up in a typically Aquarian act of passive resistance to demand equality. And it showed itself yet again near the end of 1995, at the United Nations Fourth World Conference on Women, when more than twenty-five thousand women from around the world gathered in Beijing, China, to adopt a platform for action to promote the advancement of women's human rights.

They are all shining examples of the dawning age, and in the women's conference we can see several aspects of what it will bring. The Aquarian Age will be a time for men and women to come together as one, to think of themselves as human beings, not as men or women. There is no such thing as a man being or a woman being; we are all human beings. In the Age of Aquarius, that truth becomes a reality for everyone. It is a time of integration, a time to join both of those energies within us—the yin and the yang. It also is a time for us to reevaluate our thinking about sexuality. The forward-thinking delegates at the women's conference foresaw that, including in their original platform the right to have control over and decide freely about matters of their own sexuality, including sexual and reproductive health.

But as the women proved, there are still islands of resistance to change, which is to be expected both because of the overlapping influences of the stars and the nature of humans. Once they stepped into the area of reproductive rights, they drew objections from the Vatican and countries controlled by Catholic or Islamic religious forces. The beleaguered institutions of the past stood defensively against the challenge of their dominance in that arena—this time.

But the tide has begun to rise, to sweep over and absorb those islands in the universal time of peace and unity, especially as we draw closer to the New Millennium. And even those who now resist certain aspects of change recognize its necessity and inevitability.

Pope John Paul II, as he stood before a fiftieth anniversary gathering of the United Nations, as quoted in *The New York Times*, October 6, 1995, said: "We can build in the next century and in the next millennium a civilization worthy of the human person, a true culture of freedom. We can and must do so. And in doing so, we shall see that the tears of this century have prepared the ground for a new springtime of the human spirit."

Aquarius is the time to renounce material greed and political power. Witness what is happening in the American Congress. Longtime senators and representatives are abandoning their positions, announcing they will no longer run for office. The Democratic and Republican parties are finding it harder and harder to find adherents among an electorate that is increasingly seeking a real change, a true option. The rise of an independent party movement, such as the rise of populist H. Ross Perot, is only an example of the revolutionary changes to take place under the influence of Aquarius. This is not to say that Perot or any other candidate is or is not the answer. The current offerings from within the current political structure may not prove to be the necessary ones, but they remain examples of the Aquarian cry for change.

And it is happening all over the world. Democracies have supplanted dictatorships in most of Latin America and the Caribbean. Haitians chose their first democratically elected leader in their country's history. It took the threat of invasion by a multinational force to shake loose the forces of the old order that tried to resist the change, but it happened. Then, three weeks after Uranus returned to Aquarius, Haitians—for the first time in their history—saw one democratically elected president hand over power, peacefully, to another president chosen freely by the people.

The twilight has lasted long enough. The bright light of the new day is about to shine in full force.

Humanity and unity—these are the key characteristics of Aquarius, bursting forth upon us to make everyone realize that we are all one people who deserve to live in peace, in freedom, and in harmony.

This coming age of humanity and unity is presaged in every religion and in all the different forms of astrology—from the legends of the Native Americans to the Second Coming anticipated by Christians of the world. The signs that it has begun already are echoing throughout the world.

In the legends of Native Americans, the birth of a white buffalo calf is an omen of universal significance. The Cheyenne, Sioux, and other Plains tribes believe that a White Buffalo Calf Woman once brought a sacred peace pipe to the world. Her return, they say, would signal a time of unity and goodness among people of all nations and all colors.

The odds are against it. At their peak, the American bison, or buffalo, numbered about 80 million, and the chances of a white, nonalbino, buffalo being born were about one in 10 million. Today, there are only about 130,000 buffalo.

Still, on August 20, 1994, a white buffalo calf was born on a farm in Janesville, Wisconsin. For Native Americans it was the fulfillment of their legends, as significant as the Second Coming of Christ.

Their legends also say the buffalo would change color four times in its lifetime. By the time it was a year old, the buffalo calf, named Miracle, had already changed once.

Floyd Hand, a Sioux medicine man from Pine Ridge, South Dakota, said the birth would affect all humans, not just Native Americans. "It's an omen that's bringing a change and a new world. The twenty-first century that is coming is going to unify all of us."

Far south of him, ancient Mayan prophecies similarly predicted a coming change. Using their amazingly accurate calendar cycles, the Mayans said that the spring equinox of 1995 marked the end of two 260-year cycles known as K'altun. Upon the completion of the cycles, the Mayans say, we arrive at the time when ancient and hidden knowledge is to be reawakened. They call it the end of the "age of belief" and the dawning of the Itza age, the "age of knowledge."

The prophecy was written by the Supreme Maya Council in 1475, before the arrival of the conquistadors. Almost in anticipation of the bearded conquerors from the east, the council said that a time of darkness was near at hand and that two K'altun had to pass before the Mayan solar culture would flourish again. Once the time had passed, the council predicted, Hunab K'u—God, in Mayan—would flash like lightning and pierce through the shadows that enveloped the human race. The council said that then we would begin to remember the ancient knowledge of the universe. That flood of knowledge would bring the rebirth of humanity's spirituality, and a unification of the people of the Earth in an age of peace.

On the other side of the world from the homeland of the Mayas, the same belief—that we are ending an age of darkness and entering an age of light and wisdom—is upheld in the prophecies of Indian astrology. Ages in that ancient belief stretch millions of years and are therefore impossible to pinpoint precisely. But according to various Indian astrologers, we have now reached the end of the Dark Age, the end of the spirit's descent into matter, and the end of the last of the six epochs of the Kali Yuga. Now we must pass through a final cleansing stage before the spirit once again rises in the Satva Yuga, the "age of light."

Already, we can see the points of light shining, one here and one there. They are lighting in those who will carry the message. Maybe they won't all shine at the same moment for now, but that doesn't mean they should be turned off or that they will shine any dimmer because we try to close our eyes to them. The lights are there already, shining in the darkness, lighting our way to a new tomorrow. And as more and more lights shine, they will brighten our way and brighten our world.

Take this book, then, and read on. If you have taken this book in your hand it is because the cosmic mandate is calling on you to change. Nothing comes to your hand unless it is supposed to. I don't believe in fatalism. I don't believe we have no control over our destinies. But I believe in an atunement. There

is a vibration that strikes a chord within you, calling you, awakening you to the sense that this is the first step toward what you
want, toward what you are looking for in your life.

So even to touch this book means a lot. Even to look at it
means a lot for you. The journey begins here. Where we are
going is to something brand new, something never seen before
in the history of humanity.

# 2

## The Science of the New Millennium

Some challenge astrology because the earliest astrologers placed the Earth at the center of the universe with the planets, stars, and Sun rotating around it. Because of this error in astronomy, astrology is attacked by both the pure scientist and the resolutely rational skeptic. But the Earth is our home, and while we now know that it revolves around the Sun, as do the other planets, it is the position of the Sun, the Moon, and the planets *to* the Earth that is relevant.

As the noted psychologist Carl Jung observed, we blithely accept the fact that wines are different by their vintage and the location of their vines, and for good reason. We *know* that a Chablis is different from a chardonnay, and that a 1989 chardonnay differs from its brethren of earlier and later harvests. Why should this be so? The soil and the vines remain the same. The process of wine making at a specific winery should also, we presume, remain equally the same from year to year and generation to generation. It is so that the winery's reputation is established. Yet every year, the wines of a certain region are similar to one another and different from all others; and every year, the wine of a certain field is different from the one of the year before and the one of the year to come. They are affected by the time and the place of their birth.

The skeptic will accept as much and scorn any divergence from that reality. You would be crazy to think differently. But persons too are born in different fields and at different times. They too must feel the influence of these differences or similarities. And as Jung said, this, if nothing else, lends credence to the theories of astrology—that we are each and every one different, or similar, by virtue of our time and place of birth.

But astrology is not fixed or firm. We are each and every one different, also, by virtue of ourselves and our circumstances. I do not believe that astrology is an invariable determinant of what will happen in any of our lives. Astrology is an indicator, a concentration of energies over us, that influences and affects us. And, again in the words of Jung, nothing occurs outside of its context. Everyone and everything born under certain planetary formations carries with them or it what was formed in the heavens, in the planets, and at the moment of their birth. There is a synchronization between what happens above and what happens below, on Earth, under the light of the heavens. Nothing happens above that does not have its effect below. It is such a perfect clock, a cosmic clock, that reflects on—and in—everything on Earth. It is God's perfect plan at work. As you are of the Earth, everything in the cosmos, everything astral, touches you, affects you, and serves to help you learn, grow, evolve, improve, and achieve your goals.

But you cannot expect that a child born in Calcutta, Bangladesh, or Sarajevo will have the same life as a child born to the Kennedys, even if they are born at the same precise moment in time. We are dealing with energies that flow and influence, not with the fixed and immutable. The child in Calcutta and the newborn Kennedy will share certain peaks and valleys in their lives, but they will not—cannot—be the same. That is why astrology must be analyzed in the context of an individual's circumstances. It must be passed through a filter, like a sieve, of knowing what is the reality of each individual's life.

There is ample evidence of cosmic twins—people born at the same moment in the same general area—and how their lives remain similar from birth to death, even if their circumstances set them on different planes. One well-known case involved Samuel Hemmings, a commoner, and King George III. Both were born on June 4, 1738, at almost the same moment, in the same place— St. Martin-in-the-Fields, England. Hemmings became an ironmonger and started his own business on the same October day in 1760 that George III became king. They both married on September 8, 1761. And on January 29, 1820, they both died— at the same time and of the same cause.

Similarly, Donald Chapman and Donald Brazill were born at the exact same time in two neighboring California towns on September 5, 1933. They both held similar jobs and dated girls in each other's hometown. Twenty-three years and five days after their births, on September 10, 1956, they met, and died—when they crashed head-on into each other on U.S. 101 south of Eureka, California.

What would otherwise be just bizarre coincidences take on a whole new meaning in the light of astrology. But astrology does not determine that all the same events must occur to those born at the same time, only that they are likely to.

That hypothetical child born in Calcutta at the same time as our hypothetical Kennedy may or may not be born into a family of comparative richness within Calcutta's social sphere. But, whether born to rich parents or poor ones, we will find that that child may lose one of his or her parents in a moment of tragic violence, and that the other will go on to remarry an older spouse. But maybe not, because astrology does not say that such and such will happen at a specific time of a specific day. It does not say that you must marry on a specific day or must die at a specific moment. Astrology tells us that we should be open to love at a certain time in our life and, if we are, we may find a union with the partner who will help us to be happy for the rest of our lives. Astrology tells us that on a certain day we should be careful because we are prone to accidents or surrounded by dangers, possibly devastating ones.

From there, it is up to each of us to decide what to do with that knowledge. If we close ourselves to love at a specific moment, we may eventually marry another individual, with less fortunate results. If we decide to go swimming far from shore after eating a heavy meal on the day when the stars warn us to be wary of danger in the water, we may still be saved from drowning, but it is hardly likely. Or, if we decide to stay back from the water and stand far from the shore's edge, we still could be dragged to sea by a giant tidal wave that comes out of nowhere and hauls us away. But I think that is equally unlikely. Instead, we may find that we slip in the bathtub and bang our elbow, and think to ourselves, "Ah, that is what my horoscope was warning me about."

Too many astrologers find justification for everything in the stars—after the fact. They can say that your marriage ended in divorce because your Venus was retrograde the day of your marriage. And it can be justified, because every planet has two faces, two facets, two aspects—the positive and the negative—which touch the world.

It is the same with each of us. We each have two facets, two faces. We are both shadow and light, and the day that we can accept both, when we can come to terms with our dark side instead of condemning it, we become whole. We are all both demons and angels at once. But we don't have to see those demons as something ugly, we need to make friends with them, to know them. When we know them, we can control them, placate them, and come to peace with them. By making peace with our inner demons, we can make peace with life. By knowing the two faces of the planets, we can know what to expect—both good and bad—and prepare for it.

In the New Millennium, we will make peace with our demons and with the pluralities of the planets. The two faces will be integrated. We will learn to use even the most negative energy in our favor. Knowing that today Mars is entering Scorpio, some might say, "I'm not going to work today," because Mars for many people means violence. But I say, "No, it's a beautiful, positive energy." In Scorpio, my transformation house, it means there is going to be a quantum leap, like a leap of faith, in my career or in my life—if I use it that way. It is an energy that gives me power to invent, to create; my personality will be elevated by the strength of Mars in decision making, by its aggressiveness. It is marvelous when I know how to channel the energy.

Scientific astrology will be the science of the New Millennium. The old astrology sometimes chained people, holding them down. In the new era that is dawning around us, astrology will become a tool that will guide and help us channel the energies of the heavens into our everyday lives. It becomes a map that will guide us in our travels. If I drive at night with my headlights off, I could crash into a wall or run somebody over. But if I have my lights on, I can see what lies ahead and avoid hitting anything. It is the same in life as with astrology. I will be able to orient myself better, to pick my way past the traps and make the most of the smooth runs.

In this way, astrology is like meteorology—both a science and an art. Neither is as pure a science as mathematics, for example, where every equation has but one specific outcome. The flowing masses of air and pressure zones mixed with the heat from warm water *may* turn into a hurricane—and an adept forecaster *may* correctly predict it, but only by reading the combination of atmospheric conditions and considering the *probabilities* that they will continue gathering strength and eventually turn into a hurricane. It takes a certain amount of knowledge, a certain amount of experience, and a certain amount of talent—of art—to accurately forecast the weather or a horoscope. Some of us are born with greater abilities than others, to which we add knowledge so that we can develop them into a skill, much like a great architect is born with a certain talent that he or she can learn to express by applying both the science of engineering and the art of design. But not everyone is Frank Lloyd Wright; nor is everyone Nostradamus.

Still, for those who are confused or perplexed, astrology can serve as a map to help them orient themselves better in life by understanding what is happening and why. For those who are not lost at all, astrology can serve as a guide to help them make even more use of their lives, by knowing exactly when is the precise moment to make the move they are planning. Astrology shows us why we have come to this Earth, why we are here now, and what we can do to improve ourselves. It is a dynamic potential, never a static fact. It is a map in time, of where the energies lie. Our horoscope is, simply, like an X ray of our person, through which we can know our limitations, potentialities, and what must be corrected or discarded. Our natal chart, our birth chart, is a marvelous compass to guide us on the sea of life.

Take a child, born this very moment. The formations of the planets at the instant of birth do not say this or that is a reality without possibility of change; they show us the child's potential. The seed is sown, but not grown. If that child nurtures the potential foretold in the stars, then life will not be a series of

stumblings and failed efforts, but a fruitful voyage to the summit of his or her capacity. A child born with all the planets
aligned in the highest part of his or her natal chart is bound to
reach the top—but the question becomes, "Top of what?"
Returning to the child in Calcutta again, he or she will never be
president of the United States, but may become mayor of a village or even prime minister of India.

But no matter what our horoscopes foretell, we each must take
responsibility for our actions and our lives. Too many people
blame karma, the law of cause and effect, for all the ills that
befall them. Others blame destiny. They blame God's will. Or
they blame a malefic planet, a star of nefarious intent for show-
ering them with setbacks and ill will. But there are no evil planets or unconditionally negative aspects; there are only educational
aspects, to teach us what we must know, must change, or must
correct. Destiny can be changed once the lesson is learned.

In my own case, I was born with Mercury retrograde, affecting my speech. I stuttered. According to some astrologers, that
was that. I could not speak, and never would, so I should write.
But I had other ideas, so I triumphed over the stars. I knew that
this was my area of difficulty, the area where I would have to
dedicate the most time and energy if I wanted to overcome this
deficiency. It is the same with an athlete who can run faster than
anyone but who wants to be a baseball player. The natural ability to run fast would make that person great at stealing bases,
but to be a great ballplayer, he or she also has to be able to hit
and catch. With practice, the hitting and the catching improve
to the point where that person can play baseball. If not, that
same person might consider a different sport. That's why I can
tell you, from my own personal experience, that the stars are
indicators, but their energy is not set in stone. No matter what
your birth chart says, you have the final say over how the stars
will affect you. But only if you know what they say. If not, you

are like the three blind men feeling their way around an elephant. One, holding the tail, said the elephant was long and
skinny, like a snake. The second, touching the elephant's huge
side, said, "No, it is solid and big, like a wall." And the third,
holding its trunk, said it was like a hose. If you know your natal
chart, you can see it is an elephant. You will not have to constantly wonder why certain things happened when they did; you
can see them coming and decide whether to climb onto the elephant's back for a ride or step out of its way to avoid being
trampled.

It is up to each of us to choose our course wisely. Yet for
some reason, people who would never imagine opening a new
branch for their business without studying the competition
and knowing how many potential customers they have, or
who would never think of setting out on a road trip without
first studying a map, plunge headlong through life without
ever considering the formations of the planets. Others
become trapped by fear. Rather than seeing that it is up to
each of them to channel the energy of the planets for their
benefit, they become frozen, unable to move without first
consulting their horoscopes, and unable to move if there is
the slightest hint of things going wrong. They become slaves
to the stars. But astrology is not supposed to be a trap, it is
not supposed to keep you from moving ahead with your life.
It is supposed to help you make the most of it.

You may have a terrible day ahead of you and make it turn
out beautifully, or you may have a beautiful day ahead of you
and have it turn out miserably. The day can be fine, but you are
its owner, free to ruin or enjoy all of its potential. In the same
way, you are the owner of your own life and your own destiny.
No one nor any thing can manage or manipulate your life—not
even the stars—if you are aware and alert to its possibilities. But

by knowing what is happening in the heavens above, you can know when certain hazards lie in your way. You can also know when there is an energy that is supporting you, lifting you, opening the way for you. And right now, there is a tremendous positive energy flowing into every one of our lives—the energy of Aquarius—awakening us to the possibilities of the new era, bringing amazing changes to our ways of living.

The great prophet Nostradamus predicted a period of two thousand years of peace that would begin after a time of great turmoil at the end of the millennium. It was dangerous for him to do so in the time in which he lived. Inquisitors would gladly burn anyone at the stake who even hinted that they had the ability to foresee what was to come. To the authorities of Nostradamus's time, such abilities belonged only to witches, and witches, they believed, were evil. So to hide the nature of his prophecies, Nostradamus couched them in cryptic quatrains, four-line poems, gathered together in blocks of one hundred called centuries, to be deciphered by future generations. In his poems he foretold the coming of Adolf Hitler and airplanes and missiles flying through the sky.

How did he achieve such amazing accuracy? Nostradamus described his methods in a preface to his prophecies, which he wrote as a letter to his son César. In it, he wrote that his predictions were what "the divine spirit has vouchsafed me to know by means of astronomy ... together with various secrets of the future vouchsafed to orthodox astrology." He went on to say that "things are revealed by the planetary movements."

Those same planetary movements bring the Age of Aquarius advancing upon us inevitably, exerting more and more influence upon us with each passing day. We can look to specific moments along that march to glean what will come and what the stars hold for us, but the march itself continues in spite of us, whether we study and learn from the stars or not; whether, even, we bother to look up from our world to see the great cosmic play in the heavens. It is part of the great cosmic design, the grand universal plan, of the steady advance of the great months in the great year.

The astrological ages of the Earth, known as the great months, move in reverse through the zodiac, the opposite of the advancement of the regular zodiac. Our calendar moves from Aquarius to Pisces to Aries; the Earth moves from Aries to Pisces to Aquarius.

This is so because even though the stars appear to be an immobile field of points of light fixed against the night sky, they are actually moving. The zodiac is fixed by the position of the first point of Aries on the day of the vernal equinox. Through time, the first point of Aries steps along the ecliptic, where it intersects the celestial equator, advancing through the signs of the zodiac. Hipparchus of Nicaea (c.190–c.120 B.C.) first discovered this principle, known as the precession of the equinoxes. We now know that it is due to a slight wobble in the Earth's rotation, making it so that the constellation behind the Sun at the vernal equinox changes through time.

When the first astrologers looked out at the stars and began to plot the meaning of their influence on life on this planet, Aries reigned in Aries. By the time of the birth of Christ, the first point of Aries had shifted, continuing its steady march across the cosmos, to sit within Pisces. Now, as we know, it has crossed into the Age of Aquarius, and each day this new celestial position brings increasing influence from the dominant sign of the Water Bearer.

Each tick of this great cosmic clock—the advancement of Aries through the signs of the zodiac—takes approximately 2,000 years. The full circuit through the great year, when Aries returns to Aries, takes 25,868 years. Obviously, Aries has completed this journey many times since the universe was formed and the stars began to shed their light; many times since the planets were formed and began their circuit around the Sun. And, obviously, we do not know exactly when the Earth and the other planets were born and began their heavenly march. We similarly do not know the exact time and day when the first human came into being. So we cannot devise a birth chart for Earth or its people and with it map the influences of the stars. We are limited to the history of humankind and our knowledge of it to gauge the impact of the stars and to mark the great year.

Just as each of us is influenced by both the positive and negative aspects of any sign, so too is the Earth. The opposite of our birth sign, the sign in polarity, also influences, sometimes dramatically, and sometimes only slightly. Again, it is the same with the Earth.

Also, just as the planets begin to exert their influence over the matters of Earth as they enter a sign and continue to exert their influence as they exit, so too do we begin to see the influence of both the New and Old Ages of the great year overlapping. People born in that region of time, known as the cusp of two signs, may exhibit characteristics of both. The Earth is exactly the same, except that since the ages of the great year are so long, the cuspal periods as well are long. But as each great age gives way to the next, it is marked by a revolutionary, explosive, even cataclysmic event. This dramatic event may not come exactly at the beginning or end of an age, but it comes nonetheless.

Because of this overlap of influences, it is impossible to say exactly when one age fully ends and the next fully reigns. But it is easy to see the influence of each astrological age as it played out in our history by looking closely at human development—political, social, cultural, and technological.

The earliest time we have knowledge of is the Age of Leo, around 10,000 to 8000 B.C., when early humans joined together in primitive bands and looked to the Sun, Leo's ruler, for guidance and sustenance. The Sun was fire, and for early humans gaining control over this divine power was a revolutionary technological advancement. With it, they could fend off the fearsome night and the creatures that lurked in it, cook their food, and move into caves to seek shelter from the elements. In those caves, those early humans demonstrated one of Leo's key characteristics—creativity—through the cave paintings they scratched out with primitive pigments and left behind for us to discover. Many of those paintings, we now believe, represent the desires of the artists, visualizations of what they wanted and hoped for, such as a mastodon surrounded by a fearsome hunting party bringing home food for all. The thinking behind that clearly shows Leo's polarity, Aquarius, as does the banding together itself, for Aquarius is unity and humanity.

In the Cancerian Age, from about 8000 to 6000 B.C., the Earth's primitive peoples emerged from the caves and stepped unto the fertile lands around them. This is the time of fixed dwellings, of putting down roots both literally and figuratively. In China, India, Egypt, and Mesopotamia, humans constructed shelters for themselves and slowly exchanged the feast and famine existence of the hunter-gatherers for the typically Cancerian lifestyle of the farmer. They settled the land and learned to till the soil, thus initiating the agricultural revolution that was the cultural, social, and technological development of this age. Dependent as they were on the success of the harvest—of the fertility of the land—it is small wonder that fertility rites and round, fecund female figures abounded in this period. Together they represent the strong influence of Cancer, the sign of home and motherhood, as well as that of its ruling planet, the Moon.

Around 6000 B.C., the Earth entered into the Gemini era, and the changing zodiac exerted its force on our planet, this time in the lively, intellectual, mobile, and communicative influence of the sign. The new great month saw the development of writing, from the first rough symbols etched into pottery to cuneiform and the pictogram symbols of China and Egypt. Putting down the thoughts and beliefs of their people for later generations to find and learn from demonstrated their intellectual need to record and store information. It was the great social and cultural development of the era, and coupled with the intellectual and communicative influence of Gemini, gave rise to the first groups of people coming together to be educated in what amounts to the founding of the first university systems and libraries. The Gemini tendency toward movement and physical communication showed in the technological development of the period, the first widespread use of the wheel.

Taurus is practical, reliable, and patient; filled with great powers of endurance, good in business, and possessed by a firm sense of values; loves luxury and good food; persistent, strong-willed, and determined. All of these characteristics are demonstrated in the Age of Taurus, circa 4000 B.C. The Egyptians spent generations building their great, solid, and long-lasting pyramids, which also stand as a testament to the strong influence of Taurus' polarity, Scorpio—for the pyramids are little more than elaborate coffins, overwhelmingly massive temples of death built by a society preoccupied with death and the afterlife.

By 2000 B.C. or so, the Earth moved into Aries, and its warlike influence dominated along with its Libran polarity. The wandering, warring tribes of Israel worshipped the Arian ram. The Greek civilization spread and dominated throughout the Western world, waging war upon war and crushing any opposition with its mighty military. But as they waged war with all around them, the Greeks demonstrated Libra's polar influence at home in the grace and beauty of their open, delicate temples and art. Libra's symbol is the scale, representing balance, and the balance of Greek architecture is unsurpassed. The Trojan Horse serves as a clear example of the technological development of the age in the arts of war, further reinforced by Aries' ruling planet, Mars.

Pisces may be the quintessentially clear example of an age dominated by its ruling sign. Pisces is the fish, and the fish is also the symbol of the most significant movement of the period, Christianity. The era opens about the time of the birth of Christ, who spoke of his apostles as "fishers of men." The characteristics of Pisces are humility, compassion, sympathy, sensitivity, and kindness, the same as the positive characteristics espoused in Christianity. Pisces' polarity is Virgo, the virgin, which reinforces the Christian philosophies of gentleness, humility, and charity.

But Pisces also is the battle between good and evil, between white and black, between the Europeans and the Native Americans. Pisces dominates the sea, and the Age of Pisces gives us conquests by sea and the conquistadors, who followed in the wake of Columbus to ravage the New World. As with all the ages of Earth, Pisces too cannot close without revolution, especially as Aries comes increasingly under the technological influence of Aquarius. It is only natural that the closing days of the Age of Pisces would give birth to the Industrial Revolution and that the battle between good and evil would become ever bloodier, culminating with the calculating, mechanical efficiency of the Nazis, who reveled in rockets and pure science, creating a war machine of unprecedented power. The world wars exhibit all the negative impact of worshipping technology for its own sheer power, epitomized in the single destructive flash of the atomic bomb, which stands as *the* cataclysmic event marking the transition between the ages.

In the 1960s, we felt the impact of Aquarius even more powerfully with the peace and "free love" movements of youth. The

Aquarian need for spiritual rebirth brought the resurgence of Eastern religions in the West and can be glimpsed in the misguided attempts of youth to find God through drugs.

But we are only now coming completely into the Age of Aquarius, to be increasingly dominated by our dependence on rational science, technology, and our love of space exploration. As you live it, witness the duality of the age, for Aquarius compels us with its humanity and love of science and technology; with its desire for unity and with its independence. Aquarius drives us to look within ourselves and to look to the stars, as well. This is the era of man reaching into space while joining together to protect the Earth. Aquarius is the sign of reform and of rebelliousness, of inventiveness and individuality, of unity and unconventionality. And it will influence every aspect of our lives—just as the signs of other times have influenced theirs—from sex and romance to religion and art. As we enter the final years of this millennium and approach the new, the influence of Aquarius is magnified; the planets align to intensify both the pace and the scope of change.

At the end of 1995, Pluto began its thirteen-year stay in Sagittarius, the sign that rules religion, the superior minds, laws, and publications. Sagittarius means total expansion of our minds, ourselves, and our society. Pluto is the great destroyer. But it destroys to rebuild. So, with Pluto in Sagittarius, we see the destruction of antiquated laws and rules, opening the way for a new society based on individual, responsible freedom. Pluto comes to destroy the laws that chained us and to bring the laws that free us. And with each passing day, we will see more laws become outdated, more regulations become unnecessary. As we each change into the person of the new era, a person who knows that we must respect ourselves, our fellow human beings, and our planet, regulations become unnecessary. It may seem impossible now, but we are on the verge of a time when we will not need to pass laws to protect our planet from pollution, from the dumping of toxic wastes, because each of us will consider such things inherently wrong, practically unthinkable. It may seem equally impossible now that someday we will do away with executions and death penalties, but as we each come more in tune with ourselves, we come more in tune with each other. From individuality comes unity. What is unconscionable for ourselves becomes unconscionable for all, and with that concept comes peace. So too will other laws of a bygone era fall away or be destroyed.

Sagittarius is the sign of laws. The skeleton of all the universal laws falls within its domain. But because of the duality of the zodiac, of the two faces of each sign, Sagittarius is also the sign of expansion and freedom. It is the balancing nature of the zodiac that makes it so. Unbridled freedom and expansion bring chaos and disorder. The infinite divinity of the celestial design thus provides the counterbalance within the same sign, making it the ruler of the laws that limit, that mark the territory of freedom so it does not collapse into chaos, and brings order to what would otherwise be total disorder.

Sagittarius, the centaur, half man and half horse, also rules sports, naturally. Now, as we move into the Age of Aquarius, the alignment of Pluto in Sagittarius brings us back to the realization that the old saying is true, "Sound body, sound mind." To balance all of that physical energy, there has to be a return to the spiritual as well. In India, the mystics lived in a world that was totally consumed in the spiritual; they sat marvelously—skinny, sick, and reaching for divinity. In America, people live at the other extreme, hardly sitting at all. They go for runs—run to work, run their businesses—and lose sight of the spiritual. Now the hemispheres come together. Now in the New Millennium, the two become integrated, just as the left and right hemispheres of the brain are integrated, just as our left and right hands work together.

As if it were not enough that Pluto had come to Sagittarius to do away with the old and make way for the emergence of the new, on January 12, 1996, Uranus returned to its celestial throne, Aquarius, where it is to remain for a full seven years. After years and years of transitting through the heavens, Uranus came home, signaling the commencement of the change.

Uranus is the planet of the odd, the strange, the unpredictable in everything. It is the cosmic prankster and, in its negative aspect, the cosmic pervert. Its very discovery came at the time of the French Revolution, which is fitting, for Uranus is the ruler of revolution, of breaking with everything established, everything old. Everything from fashion to human conduct changes under the influence of Uranus, especially now that it comes into full sway, and is well aspected in sextile with Pluto in Sagittarius. That sextile promises for the potential of a renewed rectitude of the human heart, reinforcing the Aquarian tendency of spirituality and humanity. Together, Pluto and Uranus are the harbingers of the new era, the powerful forces that change our very perception about our world. The most strange and odd will seem ordinary and common in these changing times. The energy of Uranus, in excellent aspect with the powerful and transforming energy of Pluto, frees humanity from the chains imposed upon us. There will be less dependency on the external, whether it be government, society, or religion. Every human being will have to become responsible for his or her own actions and decisions. Laws of the past that have no bearing on the people of today will be changed. There will be a revision and restructuring of our judicial systems.

As we move closer to the New Millennium, the influence of Pluto in Sagittarius becomes even more powerful and mystical and will intensify in 1998 when Neptune also moves into Aquarius, adding its potency to the mix in a combination of outer planets that is unprecedented in human history. We are crossing into uncharted territory for all humanity. Neptune, the planet of prisons, institutions, hospitals, artistic and religious inspiration, falls under the sway of Aquarius, just as Pluto and Uranus both are signaling a time of great upheaval. But Neptune also has the characteristics of idealism, spirituality, imagination, sensitivity, and artistic creation, all magnifying and magnified by the power of Aquarius.

These forces combined will continue to grow in influence, until on the night we end the old millennium, at the moment of midnight precisely, when it moves to eleven degrees of Sagittarius and we begin to touch divinity. On that night at the close of the old millennium and the dawning of the new, every planet will align to show us a picture of what is coming in the new era, a glimpse of what the future holds—showing us the profile of the new era of gold, the period of light and illumination, of the enlightenment of all humanity.

To make that moment when the millennia meet even more beautiful, Jupiter, the planet of luck and expansion, will be directly in Aries, indicating a new beginning, a new spring, a new way of life. Saturn will be in Taurus, an Earth sign, its own element, bringing stability to the Earth. The Moon will have just entered Scorpio, which rules the serpent of wisdom as well as the Eagle that soars to the greatest heights. The Moon comes like a psychic, a visionary, like a shaman on a mountaintop looking out onto the future. Mercury, our mind, will be entering Capricorn, where it finds stability. And Venus, the planet of love, enters on that day at zero degrees of Sagittarius, opening the door for the new era of love without chains, love that sets its own rules, love that is free of domination and control and manipulation. Mars, the planet of action, of energy, of power, of strength, of fire, will also be in Aquarius, along with Neptune, the planet of illusion, of glamour, of fancy, and of whim.

Jupiter is in a fire sign. Pluto is in fire. All of the energy inclines toward Aquarius, touching the new era that is dawning.

Until now, we have lived as automatons, sleepwalkers, believing in false idols and blindly obeying decrepit mandates. Now we are at the beginning of the dramatic awakening of consciousness in all humanity. The fire of Sagittarius and Aries makes us all more aware of the dream we have been living. Nothing, and no one, will remain the same.

But not everyone will be ready for the change. Some will resist. If all people were at the same level and were willing to progress, there would be no resistance and the change would be painless. But people fear change, people fear letting go, whether it is to death or to love. Everyone clings to what they know because they think that letting go, surrendering, means dying, means disappearing. But the change is coming whether we want it to or not, and the change will wipe the slate clean. There will be a disappearing—of what we think, what we know, and what we think we know.

# 3

## The Rehearsal Is Over;
## It's Time to Act

We are each born under and influenced by a certain sign. If you are born under the sign of Sagittarius, you are likely to be jovial, optimistic, versatile, open-minded, and freedom loving. Unfortunately, you are also likely to be prone to exaggeration, tactless, restless, and capricious. A Taurus is practical, reliable, patient, and fond of luxury and good food, as well as possessive, self-indulgent, and stubborn. The stars leave their indelible imprint on each of us, although, as I have already pointed out, we are also influenced by ourselves and our circumstances and can each work on our strengths and weaknesses if we choose. Nonetheless, despite what we may choose to do with our lives, despite what we may choose to do once we refuse to be dominated by the stars, our birth sign still makes its mark upon us. It determines the strengths and weaknesses we have to work with. It sets our positive and negative characteristics.

In the same way, the ages of the Earth make their mark upon it and humanity. But while our sign is individual in its influence, the era is for all, the age is the same for everybody. No one comes away untouched, no one escapes the influence.

Everyone who walks the face of the Earth during any given age will see, sense, feel, or know the impact of that influence. They will see it in the people around them, if not in themselves. Even if they do not recognize it as the influence of an astrological age, they will know its character. They will feel the zeitgeist, the spirit of the times, as the Germans call it.

The essence of an era is the essence of its sign. The coming Age of Aquarius is permeated, saturated, and touched by the essence, the symbolism, and all that is represented by the sign of Aquarius. The key words for Aquarius are independence and humanity. But it is also the sign of science, the sign of reform, and it is no accident that Uranus, the ruler of eccentricity and inventiveness, independence and originality, rules this sign. As the great astrologer Alan Leo said, "Aquarius is responsible for more inventions for the benefit of humanity than any of the other signs."

Aquarius is the Water Bearer, pouring knowledge over the Earth. Its symbol can be seen as flowing water, as electricity, as the air, which is everywhere, because Aquarius is an air sign.

The Age of Pisces was the age of the sea and land. But Aquarius, the air sign with the love of both technology and freedom, signifies space exploration, of intergalactic travels, of reaching out beyond our small planet into the vast universe. Aquarians are filled with intellectual curiosity and the age is no different. We will be compelled to discover, to seek knowledge in ourselves, at home, on Earth, in space, wherever.

Like the air, which is free to move where it will, Aquarius is a freedom-loving sign—"as free as the wind." The new era, the New Millennium, brings with it an era of light and freedom. For too many years people have been "free" in quotes, "free" in name only, "free" within certain restrictions, which is not free at all. We have been "free" if we could produce the proper documents, but have been, in fact, at liberty, which is very different from being truly free. We have been merely loose as long as we obeyed certain rules, adhered to certain regulations, and maintained certain socially acceptable behaviors.

These rules and regulations have been imposed on us, and we have become dependent upon them. We expect others to tell us how to behave, how to act, and in many cases, how to think. We have become reliant on having others tell us that what we are wearing looks good, that what we said is, in fact, a good idea. But to be free means not being dependent on anyone or anything. Being free means being independent. Being truly free means being like an animal in the jungle that depends on no one. It obeys only the laws of nature to survive and thrive.

In the coming age, people will unite with nature and with their own natures, too. We will not look to others to dictate for us what is correct. Others will not decide what is fashionable to wear. Nor will they want to. We each will feel confident in our own choices and confident in each other's ability to decide for ourselves. We will be free of our dependency on gaining the approval of others. We have spent our lives rehearsing for life, trying on different costumes and taking on different roles, all the while seeking the approval of our peers, waiting for the "directors" of our lives to tell us we have played our part well. Now, we will shed our masks and costumes, to live and feel and touch and know. The rehearsal is over, it's time to act.

This will be a challenge for us on many levels. It is hard to give up our dependencies, hard to make a decision without looking to others to tell us that we've made the right choice. And it will be hard for others to accept that we can and will make these decisions for ourselves. True freedom challenges all of our institutions, our laws, our religious edicts, which exist only to mark the limits of our freedom, to tell us what is right and wrong. But in the Age of Aquarius we won't need others to define those limits for us. We each, individually and collectively, will know right from wrong.

This does not mean a descent into lawlessness, but as we move into an era of increasing individuality, spirituality, and a sincere humane respect for the rights of all, we will, in fact, answer to a higher authority—ourselves. What will be torn away are laws that infringe on that authority, that breach our individual and universal sense of morality, of right and wrong. We all know it is wrong to impose our will on another person or for them to impose their will on us. No law can make it right. In the coming age, any law designed for controlling, for dominating, will be destroyed, rewritten, changed. Laws that permit one group of people to impose their will on another group by virtue of race, religion, or any other reason will be similarly destroyed.

In the Age of Pisces, we had masters and slaves, black and white, left and right. Pisces is two-sided. Aquarius is flowing air and water, like the circulation of our blood, going everywhere equally.

The new era is an era of hope, happiness, optimism, and constructive revolution. It is a time of nonconformity, of not conforming to what has been, to begin inventing or reinventing the new life. Originality is a sacred word of the new age. We are obligated to originality. It is the time of positive individuality—not of egoism, but of recognizing and respecting individuality in yourself and others. It is the time of antitraditionalism, innovation, friendship, and Love with a capital "L."

Our personal and global unions will change. Men and women will no longer join in a mere physical bond. Each of us will seek our spiritual twin and join in a union that goes beyond the flesh. Integration and unity are key words of the New Age, a time for joining together at the individual and global levels. The time has come to put aside the traditional concepts of unions, of husband and wife, for true partnerships based on all-embracing friendship and true love. We will find ourselves looking more and more beyond physical notions of beauty, as these too are shattered under the influence of Aquarius, to get ever nearer to bonds based on the compatible joining of kindred spirits. Outdated concepts of dominance and subservience shatter against the Aquarian characteristics of humanity and independence. We will not be bonded to each other by pieces of paper, legal documents, or by the blessings of strangers, but by our own desire to be together. The old chains disappear and we stay together because that is where we want to be out of true love. Nothing can be held against its will, because at the very least it will wither and die. This is true of love as well. Love cannot be made to exist because a document or a band of gold makes it so. Love exists from within our hearts and keeps us joined because it is mutual and unconditional. We will love both our individuality and the individual we share it with.

We will be free to love and to be loved. We will love ourselves and all around us, we will be free to enjoy ourselves—truly free, without feeling guilty. Too many of us believe that we don't deserve to have fun, don't deserve to have pleasure. So when we do find pleasure, we can't enjoy it because we're too busy feeling guilty to savor the moment. That is ridiculous. Pluto has returned to Sagittarius and remains there through the turn of the century into the New Millennium. It is the time to find joy in yourself and in all around you.

Sagittarius is the sign of the spontaneous joy of life, of finding pleasure in what we have, not in what we don't; of taking time to relish the beauty and abundance around us, be it the particular blue of the sky at a specific moment, the soothing sound of the rainfall washing down upon us, or the quiet pleasure of sharing a peaceful moment without words with the ones we love.

In the Age of Aquarius, we want to enjoy the trip as much as the destination. There never seems to be enough time for everything we have to do. But in the coming age we will make the time, take the time, and enjoy life. We won't feel that everything is a race or that we are constantly competing. If you're always competing, you wind up bitter because you're always trying to beat somebody, to be better than somebody, and there always seems someone else to be better than, even if it is only to become better than yourself. In that race, you lose. What's important is not to get there, but to get there happily, in harmony, and at peace.

The New Millennium shall be a time of plenty because no one deserves to be poor, no one is destined to be poor. That is a concept that comes from the Age of Pisces—that some are destined to be poor in life because they are poor in spirit. The New Age is a time of prosperity in life, in love, and in all. It is the eternal springtime of the spirit and it brings an exuberant flowering of new ideas. The new person of the New Age must be truly rich, not just rich in material things, but rich in health, in knowledge, in spirit, and in sex.

In the Age of Aquarius, what is important is not to have, but to be. We have concentrated too much on external things, forgotten that we have souls. We have been totally unconscious to what is of the inner life. But the proliferation of material greed, political power, and racial discrimination now crumbles before the spiritual rebirth, which forces us to look inward for the principles that force us to uphold the renewed ideals of love, honor, and truth. The children who are born now in the time of Aquarius no longer want to *believe*, they want to *know*. Knowing for ourselves—personal knowledge that goes beyond a mere belief in the words of others—is a sacred principle of the Age of Aquarius. We go beyond faith to find truth.

Rules and institutions will crumble under the weight of this scrutiny. Laws, politics, and even religions will be tested, altered, or devastated by the profound examination that already has begun. We will discard the sacred texts of yesterday and write them anew with new knowledge and new vision. This does not mean an end to religion; it means taboos and dogmas will be cast aside. We will find that the Second Coming of Christ comes from within us, not necessarily in the actual coming of the one Son of God. It is the awakening of Christ in yourself and in each of us. The Ten Commandments are excellent rules of goodness, but we must take them into our hearts, make them a part of us. When you have internal peace, you won't violate any of the Commandments. Under Aquarius, we will come to understand our own internal book. We will understand the Bible and the Koran and all the holy writings because we will come to touch our own interior well of knowledge. We will *know* what is right without having to look to an outside list of rules to tell us how to behave.

The doctrines and dogmas of the past will be destroyed, but our belief in God will not. Doctrines and dogmas will be replaced by true faith in ourselves and in our knowledge. We will not say we have faith because someone tells us it is so. We will have faith because we know for ourselves what is real and what is true and what is not.

We are growing ever closer to the much heralded global village, into a united society which will not be divided by "isms"—not communism, socialism, or capitalism.

The New Millennium is the time for us to touch and be touched by the stars. It is the time for us to reach into and beyond ourselves. It is the time for a new way of thinking to go hand in hand with the new era. And it is inevitable. It is a time of respecting one another because we know ourselves better. It is the time to shed the shackles of bigotry and hatred; the time to denounce sexism and chauvinism; the time to renounce material greed and political power.

Protecting the environment here on planet Earth takes on increasing emphasis and importance as we move deeper into the era of Aquarius. Scientists estimate that at the current rate of destruction, humans will push an average of one hundred species of plants and animals to extinction *every day*, nearly a thousand times faster than the rate that existed from prehistory to the present.

The rain forest in the Brazilian state of Rondônia once stood majestically and unspoiled in the lush region south of the Amazon, its two-hundred-foot-tall trees spreading thickly like an unbroken emerald carpet, filled with the sounds of proliferating wildlife. Then, in the 1970s, settlers swept in, slashing and burning huge swaths through the forest in a frenzied rush that carved out massive tracts of land for roads and towns. Now, one fifth of the Rondonian rain forest is gone; at present rates of destruction, the forest itself will be completely wiped out within twenty-five years.

In Madagascar, more than 90 percent of the original plant life has vanished. Villagers searching for firewood and building materials in the foothills of the Himalayas and throughout Haiti have virtually eliminated the trees and the forests that once existed there. Some scientists estimate that at least 12 percent of the birds in the Amazon basin and 15 percent of the plants in Central and South America will die no matter what preventative measures are taken. Even in the United States, 95 percent of the virgin forests that stood when the first pilgrims landed over 300 years ago has since been destroyed. Also, the Environmental Protection Agency estimates that the continental United States has lost roughly half of its wetlands.

And in many cases we have no idea what is being lost. The plants that still exist are disappearing faster than scientists can discover them. "It's as though the nations of the world decided to burn their libraries without bothering to see what is in them," University of Pennsylvania biologist Daniel Janzen said at a *Time* magazine conference. He means that of an estimated 5 to 30 million different forms of life on Earth, scientists have recorded only 1.7 million. Yet that relatively small amount has yielded tremendous benefits. About one fourth of the pharmaceutical drugs in use in the United States contain ingredients that came originally from wild plants. What cures remain in the wild waiting to be discovered, or to be destroyed before we get to them? It is literally a race for life, a race that some who have felt the increasing influence of the New Age have already joined.

Environmental "green" movements are proliferating and concern for the rain forest is growing. Environmentalists recognize that the rain forest serves as the lungs of the Earth, cleansing the carbon dioxide that humans and animals expel into the atmosphere, breathing out the life-giving oxygen we all so desperately need. To kill the forest is to kill ourselves, and the people who have been touched by the spirit of the New Millennium already have seen this. Like deft doctors racing to defeat a deadly epidemic, they are rushing to stop the destruction that is destroying the rain forest like a fast-spreading cancer. These people are truly the doctors of planet Earth, seeking a cure for the destruction already done while at the same time sharing their wisdom with the rest of us, trying to teach us how to avoid further spread of the disease, trying to teach us how to avoid killing ourselves.

These are all elements of the influence of Aquarius. Again, it is a function of the Water Bearer's duality. As we reach out to the planets and stars, we grow more concerned about the planet of our birth. Aquarius is an air sign and, therefore, it is only natural that we would reach into the sky; and as water is the sustenance of all life on Earth so will Aquarius demand that we protect our home planet.

In Greek mythology, Uranus was both son and husband of Gaia, the goddess of the Earth. As Uranus, the planet, reenters Aquarius almost at the start of the New Millennium, this sense of being both the children and the partner of our planet is reborn, and a new spirit of caring for Mother Earth and working in conjunction with her without despoiling her are similarly reborn.

The children of the New Age, those already born and those to be born, will take up environmental movements with renewed vigor. Already the seeds of this revolution are planted. But as we move deeper into the new era, this inclination turns to passion and youth rejects consumer culture and returns to the wilderness or to space.

A precursor to this Aquarian trend already exists. The Findhorn Foundation sprang up in 1962 a mile from the fishing village of Findhorn, in Morayshire, northeast Scotland. There, Peter and Eileen Caddy and Dorothy Maclean established a community dedicated to the advancement of religion and the conservation and preservation of the natural world. Their techniques are founded on the need to apply spiritual principles to everyday life, to commune with nature on a spiritual and practical level meant to preserve it, and to apply those principles in the construction of ecologically sound housing, renewable energy sources, recycling, and organic gardening. Proven successful, the techniques have been adopted by other communities and individuals around the world. Major cities from Seattle to Miami have now developed recycling programs aimed at cutting down on the mountains of waste by reusing, or finding new uses for, what was previously discarded.

As we become more in tune with our planet and our place in its complex ecological system, we will not only learn new ways to care for the Earth, but also ways to care for ourselves. Fully recognizing that we are all interconnected with each other and with our planet, we will recognize that to care for the Earth requires also for us to take care not to overburden it. The religious dictate to "go forth and multiply" has disastrous effects on the ecosystem. Overpopulation is a devastating disease for nature and for us. In the wild, nature has its own often harsh checks and balances to prevent unrestricted population growth. Overpopulation of a herd of deer brings about the death of the herd by starvation when they overgraze their environment. Too many lions in a pride brings an overkill of other animals, creating an imbalance of the delicate food chain. The pride must then split up, move on, or die. The problem with moving on is that sooner or later, there will be no place to move on to, which is the problem facing humanity. We have used our intelligence to defeat most of the naturally occurring checks and balances, only to find ourselves destroying the very heart of the system— the planet itself.

The only answer is to use our intelligence to defeat this ultimate end by controlling our own population growth. Religious bans on birth control must therefore be considered in the light of a new reality. Preventing conception through artificial means can no longer be considered sacrilegious; it must be considered sacred. Restraint in matters of procreation is, in this sense, the most profound display of fraternal love and compassion for all humanity, because it is a personal commitment to protecting our planet and all the people on it. Controlling the growth of the human population ensures plenty for all, and ensures the survival of the Earth. It is morally wrong to act as though we are separate from nature and from the Earth, and our religious leaders too will have to recognize that the biblical dictate to be fruitful and multiply is meant to be applied in its spiritual, not physical, sense; and that the Commandment "Thou shalt not kill" applies to our mother planet as well as to all on it.

As our connection to and interconnection with nature and one another becomes increasingly clear in the New Millennium, medicine too will change. We will discard outdated forms of medicine, discovering that we grow ill first in our souls, then in our minds, and then in our bodies. In our new communion with nature, we will find cures to diseases in heretofore unknown plants and herbs. We will become partners with our doctors in our own health, taking into our hearts the global concepts of preservation, of preventing destruction before it occurs, of curing ourselves every day before we become ill.

In the Age of Pisces, the age of either/or, we exalted science for its own sake as the savior of the race and planet. By solely embracing science, we attempted to kill God, or at least the concept of God. Science had an explanation for everything and challenged our most basic religious beliefs as the discoveries compounded one upon another and scientists gave increasingly complex explanations for all "natural" phenomena. Science, however, is a double-edged sword, wielded as much to prove as to disprove, or to demand a standard of proof higher for the matters of the spirit than for the purely physical. Sir Isaac Newton is remembered as the father of differential calculus, the discoverer of the law of gravity, and founder of Newtonian physics. But no pure scientist of today wishes to be reminded that Newton was a devout believer in astrology, based on the principles of Johannes Kepler before him. And if they are reminded, they easily dismiss the fact as a quirk of genius, in much the same way that Albert Einstein never bothered to comb his hair.

Yet today scientists are returning to a sense of a force that is beyond their ability to measure, beyond their experiments. It should be so at this specific moment in time because Aquarius is both the sign of technology and spirituality. The Aquarian Age is the time for the integration of science and spirituality, for the reconciliation of science and religion.

For example, most of today's astronomers and physicists accept that the universe was born in a single explosive instant from an infinitesimally small pinpoint of energy, popularly known as the big bang theory. After the initial explosion, it took hundreds of thousands of years for the first atoms to form and for the universe to cool enough for photons to escape, radiating throughout the entirety of the universe and bathing it in light, that moment which the Bible refers to as the creator saying, "Let there be light." Billions of years later, the scientists say, the first generation of stars exhausted most of their hydrogen fuel. Some of them collapsed and exploded, creating the heavier elements such as carbon, oxygen, iron, and uranium—the stuff of life. These base elements make up every known form of life in the universe, including us. We are a living, breathing part of the universe, connected to it in ways we do not yet understand.

"We are all literally made up of stardust," said astronomer George Smoot of the University of California's Space Sciences Laboratory and author of *Wrinkles in Time*. This much we know. But where that first pinpoint of intense energy came from— what unleashed its force to explode outward over billions of light-years of space; what set that power loose to evolve over the billions of years since into the intricately interconnected system of planets and stars; what brilliant design could set forth the pattern of development that could bring as complex a structure as humans into being—the scientists cannot explain or are uncomfortable explaining because it requires them to suddenly trade their theories and facts for the possibility that a supreme force beyond their explanations set it all in motion for a purpose.

"Facing this, the ultimate question challenges our faith in the power of science to find explanations of nature," Smoot wrote. "Is this then where scientific explanation breaks down and God takes over?"

In this synthesis of science and spirituality in the Age of Aquarius, technology explodes. Aquarius and Aquarians love technology. Little surprise then that computers have become the dominant influence of the end of the twentieth century, enhancing our capacity for knowledge and connecting us in the Aquarian sense of unity that shrinks borders and takes us closer to Marshall McLuhan's concept of a "global village." We are interconnected through computers in a network that spans the world and speeds us into the information revolution, easing our access to knowledge and pushing us to redefine our social, political, and economic structures. These same machines that made it possible for humans to walk on the Moon and take their first tentative steps toward exploring the stars are making their way beyond our businesses, into our schools and our homes. Seniors and toddlers alike speak of "surfing the Internet," letting their computers take them wherever their imaginations wish to go.

As the connections grow and the access to computers increases until virtually every man, woman, and child uses one, we will reach across the globe as easily as—more easily than— we now cross the street. We will know our neighbors in Bangladesh as well as we know those in our immediate neighborhood. And we will find our differences shrinking, our global consciousness growing. This is the natural linking of technology and humanity, to bring about increasing unity. The information revolution, then, is just that: a revolutionary way of attaining information and a revolutionary way of using it. Knowledge is power, we are told, and the quest for knowledge in the Age of Aquarius will lead us to find the power within ourselves to help us believe in ourselves.

As children become accustomed to computers in the classroom, antiquated methods of education will be thrown out. Concepts considered fundamental to teaching in years past will become archaic, outmoded, and come crashing down. True knowledge is not given to anyone, it is gained individually. True knowledge implies thinking about what we know, rather than a mere accumulation of facts. Which does more good, to know that the Inquisition lasted officially from 1283 to the late 1500s? Or that it perverted Christian philosophy as a means of exerting power?

The advance of technology and the access to information will help make true knowledge more possible for all, and the accelerating pace of technological advances will free us to seek higher knowledge. Our classrooms will move outdoors, into gardens, where concepts can be considered and applied, and the constricting walls of schoolhouses will give way to a modern return to the open-air institutes of Aristotle. We will devote more time to finding the natural talents of each individual, rather than forcing them to retain thousands of dates they will never use again. We will find the joy of learning once again.

But our minds will not only be expanded with what we now consider to be knowledge. In the New Millennium, the Age of Aquarius, our mental powers expand in ways we have only glimpsed in the past. Neptune reigns over the thalamus and mental and nervous processes. Pluto is associated with the creative and regenerative forces of the body, as well as with the unconscious. Sagittarius signifies expansion and the "higher mind" of human beings. Aquarius and its ruler, Uranus, are associated with physical changes and the intellect. ESP, astral projections, telepathy, and clairvoyance—all forms of parapsychology—evolve to fruition with our expanded capacities. What seemed wondrous or impossible before becomes possible in the New Age. Nonbelievers are forced to believe as they witness what before seemed incredible. We will come to know these as natural laws, which now, because we do not yet understand them, are called occult powers, mystical, or are attributed to forces outside of ourselves.

If this seems far-fetched, think of how many miracles have come to pass already. Who a mere hundred years ago would have imagined that humans would walk on the face of the Moon or spend extended periods of time floating far above our atmosphere, circling the Earth in space stations? Who in the time of Abraham Lincoln would have imagined us replacing a diseased human heart with a mechanical one to extend the life of a person previously doomed to die? And who as recently as the time of Prohibition would have imagined us harnessing the power of the atom to produce the most devastatingly destructive bomb in human history? Or using the same power as fuel to light our biggest cities? Or using a light beam—the laser—to perform microscopic surgery?

All would seem impossible to a person just a few short decades ago. Take a person from any of those times and transport them into our present, and they would cry a thousand times over things we consider mundane, "It's a miracle." Surely, these are all technological advances, but humans have evolved beyond the capabilities of their forebears as well. Our average life expectancy today is close to twice what it was just a century or two ago. Humans run faster and jump farther than they ever have, as we see every time an Olympic record is shattered, and they will continue to do so. The sum average of individual knowledge for any child of today in a developed society is far beyond what it was for the average adult in any of what would be considered advanced societies 150 years ago.

Is it far-fetched, then, to believe that our evolution will continue, and that our mental powers will expand in ways we cannot even imagine today? It shouldn't be.

The explosive expansion of what today is known as our paranormal capacity is evidenced in the lay of the stars for the coming age and in the Bible. In Joel 2:28 it is written that "And it shall come to pass afterward, that I will pour out my spirit on all flesh; your sons and your daughters shall prophesy, your old men shall dream dreams, your young men shall see visions."

That time has come.

The devout Catholic, skilled doctor, and unparalleled prophet Nostradamus also foresaw an incredible development of our abilities in the New Millennium. Applying what he called celestial science, Nostradamus foretold of an era of enlightenment, in which science and religion are united and people are able to free their inner selves and open themselves up to the higher powers and levels of the universe.

In his native French, Nostradamus wrote that "The divine word will give to the substance that which contains heaven and earth, occult gold in the mystic deed. Body, soul, and spirit are all powerful. Everything is beneath his feet, as at the seat of heaven."

Although obscured to evade the persecutions of the Inquisitors during his lifetime, the words are now interpreted to mean that the divine force pours knowledge and enlightenment down on the Earth and its people. The discoveries thus made available to all encourage the development of mental powers. Anything will seem possible in the climate of a greater unity of mind, soul, body, and emotions. People will be able to manipulate the basic forces of the universe in a way that will seem utterly fantastic to those not involved with it.

Nostradamus also predicted a great "time of trouble" at the close of the millennium, a time of destruction and of a great war. That this indeed shall come to pass is likely not only because of the amazing accuracy of his prophecies, but because of the alignment of the planets at that time. The destructive force of Pluto, which makes room for renovation by destroying what has been, is now and will continue to be magnified in Sagittarius as we cross into the New Millennium. But whether or not the worst of the events Nostradamus foretold come to pass, he saw that there would be a great spiritual rebirth throughout the world. Individuals will renounce the falsehoods of materialism and look inside themselves. After communication is restored, people will come to this realization together, and there will be a great rebirth of philosophy that blends the Eastern and Western religions. It will be a worldwide movement upholding the truth as everyone perceives it, just as is to be expected in the Age of Aquarius. This time of healing will usher in a more spiritually mature age, and people will be able to heal themselves and the world.

Also in keeping with what the alignment of planets presages for the New Millennium, Nostradamus predicts the tearing down of past institutions, including the mighty religions of the Age of Pisces. "Temples consecrated in the early Roman fashion," he wrote, "will reject the broken foundations; taking their early human laws, expelling almost all the cults of the saints."

Some also interpret his words to mean that the feminine aspects of God, which have been ignored, neglected, and reviled for the entirety of the Age of Pisces, will again be recognized and revered. This too is a return to the early ages of humanity and ancient societies in which the female aspect of God was worshipped and adored. During the patriarchal era of Pisces, the female aspect was suppressed and repressed. Now society will come to terms with the divinity of both masculine and feminine aspects, of Mother Earth and Father Sky, of yin and yang, and of the synthesis of energies for a more balanced worldview.

Following the time of trouble, there also will be a "green" revolution, in part to reclaim the lands damaged at the close of the century and as a continuation of the ecological movements of today. People will live in extended families beyond the nuclear families of today, and their communities will be Earth and ecology conscious.

Slipping into a trancelike state just before his death, the great Russian author Leo Tolstoy also spoke of a tremendous change coming sometime in the future. "I see the passing show of the world drama in its present form, how it fades like the glow of evening on the mountains," he said. He spoke of a "class war in America" followed by "a time when the world will have no use for armies, hypocritical religions, and degenerate art."

We are indeed at the time for the total destruction of the old, before the time of rebirth. It is a time of earthquakes brought about by the cathartic conjunctions of planets exerting their powerful pull on the Earth. If the tiny Moon, Earth's only satellite, with its minuscule gravitational pull, is able to move whole oceans, to make the tides come and go around the globe, imagine the force on the Earth of these planets combining the magnetic strength of their gravitational fields.

But the time of trouble is brought on by more than just the physical effect of gravity. In astrological terms, we live in the time that Pluto, the unappeasable Roman god of death, the great destroyer, the planet that rules over crime and the underworld, combines with the expanding influence of Sagittarius; and Uranus, the planet of upheaval and revolution, enters its celestial place of sovereignty, Aquarius. Thus the potential for increasing crime and violence in the streets, mass suicides by adherents of doomsday cults, rebellion, revolution, and even war are augured by the incredible celestial orientation of the planets.

There will be conflict and it is necessary that there be conflict for the renewal to begin, but we need not fear. There is nothing we can do to prevent it, but just as we can learn to use the stars and our horoscopes as maps, as guides, to illuminate our way so that we can avoid danger and make the most of our lives, we can also learn to recognize the death throes of the old age for what they are, to see them coming, and to prepare ourselves to go beyond them into the golden era of lasting peace that is to follow.

# 4

## The Death of the Old Age

The twisted ways, twisted ideas, and negative energies are exaggerated in the final years of one millennium and the start of a new. They are like the death throes of a dying animal that twists upon itself, contorting against the pain, refusing to go peacefully, releasing in its rage all that is grotesque. As with the animal, all the worst of the era is magnified in a final flash of fury. The despicable, the reprehensible, the loathsome, and the vile all boil to the surface to concentrate in poisonous pools before they are dried up by the blaze of the incoming age.

Every age of the Earth begins with a revolutionary, evolutionary event and ends with a cataclysmic, apocalyptic event. Christ was born, signaling the start of the Age of Pisces; Christ was killed, as the defenders of the previous age, the Age of Aries, raged against its death. The Roman Empire sank into debauchery and violent spectacles. The new Christians were pitted against lions in the Colosseum. And Nero, who instituted the persecution of the Christians, fiddled as Rome and the Age of Aries burned.

The event signaling the end of the Age of Pisces, the last days of the Sun of the Piscean Age, happened on August 6, 1945, at Hiroshima, Japan. It had been ushered in just three weeks earlier, when the first atomic bomb was detonated in an experimental explosion in the New Mexico desert. Seeing its destructive power, the scientist J. Robert Oppenheimer quoted from the Bhagavad-Gita: "I am come. And I am death." But using the bomb against the Japanese—in a sudden, surprising, explosive blast that killed or injured more than one hundred thousand—was the worst single act of violence in human history, the supreme moment of destruction by brother against brother, and it shrieked loudly the death of the Age of Pisces. It was the climactic event signaling the closing of the era, the worst the age could unleash; but just as the climax of a movie comes a short time before its actual end, so too did the climax and end of Pisces. The violence and suffering that we see around us is what remains of the age, before we emerge in the golden era of peace and unity.

The whole of the Piscean Age stands as the age of contrasts, of the constant struggle between opposing forces, of the battle between good and evil, black and white, left and right. It began roughly about the time of Christ's birth and, as with any age, the essence of its sign shaped the essence of the age.

Pisces is the sign of the twin fish of the zodiac. Piscean traits are humility, compassion, sympathy, unworldliness, and sensitivity. But it has two sides, two feet firmly planted. It divides between ugly and pretty, good and bad, black and white, Roman and Christian. Pisces, naturally, is a water sign, and the age was the age of the sea, when Europeans sent their ships across the ocean, setting sail for the New World on voyages of discovery and conquest. Thus it became the age of conquest by sea, of conquistadors dominating the natives of the New World.

Still, there is no more significant movement within the age than the foundation and development of Christianity. The symbol of the fish became the symbol of the new religion, painted in the catacombs of early Christians. Christ was the "fisher of souls," and showed himself to his disciples after his death with the miracle of the fishes. And, through his teachings, Christ displayed all the most positive of the Piscean traits, the humility, the compassion, the sympathy. But Pisces also is the symbol of martyrdom and pain, as can be seen in the myth behind the constellation. According to Roman mythology, Venus and Cupid, terrified by the giant Typhon, hurled themselves into the river Euphrates and became fishes.

Christ, of course, became a martyr as well, making the ultimate sacrifice for humanity by giving his life on the Cross. But although Christ's birth and the religion founded in his name were Piscean, Christ himself was Aquarian in nature. Aquarians by nature are iconoclasts, rule breakers, rebels, and independent idealists who readily transgress against the codes of conformist culture. Christ, perhaps more than any other in our history, was obviously a rebel who transgressed against the rules of his time in the name of idealism, humanity, and compassion. He chose well the day of his entry into the city of Jerusalem, the day of the Passover feast, producing the reaction that would lead to his Crucifixion.

Christ's actual birth sign is open to debate. No one is really certain of the year he was born, much less the day. Although we celebrate his birth on December 25, no one really knows for sure, and the day of celebration, Christmas, appears to have been picked to coincide with ancient Roman Bacchanalian festivals; or, with even more ancient celebrations of the winter solstice, the changing of the seasons from fall to winter. Still, based on our knowledge of astronomical events that may account for the brilliant star of Bethlehem, arguments have been made that Christ may actually have been born in the early days of April, making him an Aries. Although some would argue that the forceful, sometimes even pugnacious character of Aries is hardly fitting of Christ's humble, peaceful character, the more positive traits of Aries easily could account for his pioneering spirit and courage. Aries is the torchbearer of new ideas, willing to take risks, enterprising and direct.

Similarly, Siddhartha Gautama, the Buddha, is thought to be an Arian by birth, although some say he was a Taurean. Whichever, he had an Aquarian soul, and his mission to bring peace and enlightenment to the world predated Christ's by some five hundred years. Buddha, which in Sanskrit means "enlightened one," was the son of the ruler of a petty kingdom. He was raised in sheltered luxury, but at the age of twenty-nine realized the emptiness of the life he had come to know and set out on a journey, a quest, to seek illumination. His discovery and subsequent teachings brought him into conflict with the dominant religion of his time, Hinduism, believing that anyone should be admitted regardless of caste.

After his death, differing interpretations of his teachings brought several conflicting schools of thought into being. About the time of Christ's birth and the start of the Age of Pisces, the Mahayana doctrine developed, and although no one even knows the names of its founders, it became one of the most potent philosophies. In it, the human Buddha who walked the Earth gathering followers and founded the religion was but the corporeal incarnation of the Buddha nature, similar to the Son of God in Christianity. And as Buddhism spread throughout the world, its followers became the subjects of persecution, as were the Christians, time and again.

Later still, in the second half of this final century of the millennium, Bhagwan Shree Rajneesh stepped forward as a transgressor against what had been, to illuminate the way into the next millennium. Bhagwan, who in later years was called Osho, was born in Kuchwada, Madhya Pradesh, India, on December 11, 1931. At the age of twenty-one, he became enlightened and began developing his dynamic meditation techniques, which would lead to a "new man." His message, he said, was "a science of transformation"; his aim, "to melt all systems of thought ... so that a new kind of warmth surrounds the earth." He openly challenged religious leaders to public debates and had his life threatened repeatedly. His attempt at building a commune in a U.S. desert, a flowering oasis in the midst of barrenness, brought antagonism from other groups and he was forced to leave after four years. His followers say he never died, but "left his body" on January 19, 1990.

Buddha may have been an Aquarian in nature sent to light the way for future generations, and Osho came much later, but it is Christ's birth that signals the start of the Age of Pisces. Christ's teachings uphold the fundamental Piscean characteristics of humility and compassion. But both his teachings and his sacrifice were perverted repeatedly into weapons used to blackmail and intimidate, as the Piscean Age showed its dark side. Crusaders fought "holy wars" in the name of the church. Inquisitors sent so-called heretics to their deaths. Native Americans who refused to convert, to adopt the religion of the Old World, were burned at the stake by Spanish priests. These zealots called what they did evangelizing, but it was in fact an attempt to destroy a religion that was founded in the authentic contact between people and God, between people and nature. Those who lived in that purity, in that contact, in that fraternity, were attacked by the newcomers, enslaved, and forced to abandon their ways of old.

The conquistadors were driven by greed to seek out adventure in the newly discovered lands of the west. For them, the quest for gold justified their atrocities, their ruthlessness, and their treachery. Their homeland was still relatively fresh from the battles with the Moors, the battles over the Holy Land, in a clear-cut fight of blacks against whites, both fighting in the name of God. Rather than seeing their ways as two sides of the same coin, and rather than listening to the very precepts of their own religion and its admonitions against killing, Saracens and Christians warred in crusade after crusade for control of Jerusalem and its surrounding lands. Two hundred years later, as the conquistadors launched their ships, they were in the final days of the Inquisition, still filled with a religious fervor that permitted gross abuses of Christ's message that permitted gross inhumanities in the name of God.

As they stepped onto the fresh—and to them, virgin—lands of the New World, they came face to face with a culture that found its deities in nature and in the heavens. The Mayan kings were the earthly representatives of the Gods, ruling with divine grace. Mayan astrology was a greatly advanced art and science, with a calendar far more accurate than that of those who came to conquer. In fact, Mayan mythology told of the coming of the men on the sea, but it mistakenly conferred upon them the status of gods. And, despite the efforts of the Mayas to extend every hospitality to the newcomers, the conquistadors soon showed their bestial lust for wealth and their propensity for violence by turning on their hosts and opening the way for the wave upon wave of brutality that would follow.

Every sign has two faces, the positive and the negative. Pisces is characterized by humility and unworldliness—the dismissal of worldly things. The conquistadors exemplified arrogance and avarice. Following in their wake, Pilgrims and Puritans both showed the excesses of the Piscean Age as they pushed the Native Americans from their land, and later launched the infamous witch hunts.

The latter is a natural extension of the Piscean concept of good and evil, of domination and subjugation—whether it be a people or a passion. Christ spoke of eternal love; the churches spoke of eternal sin. Christ spoke of salvation; the churches spoke of damnation. The emphasis went from doing good for its own sake to doing good to avoid burning for all eternity in the fires of hell. We were taught that we could purify our souls by punishing our bodies. At its most frenzied, less thought was given to good than to the avoidance of evil, at any cost.

This is not to condemn the churches or the organized religions, which have all done their good. If not for religion, we would have long ago blown ourselves up in a war for nothing more than greed. Modern religion awakened our spirituality, gave us universal concepts of good and evil to consider, rather than a panoply of deities to choose from as we pleased to justify our every action.

But the concept of guilt, of sin, became in too many cases a tool for personal power. Inquisitors used it to silence those called "heretics," so loosely defined a term that it could be applied to almost anyone who questioned. In 1633, an inquisitional tribunal sentenced the great astronomer Galileo to life imprisonment for defending the Copernican theory that the Earth revolved around the Sun, rather than vice versa. Countless others were imprisoned or executed for the "crime" of differing with the Church.

Any age has its excesses; Pisces was no different. Every age also has its good; again, Pisces was no different. But it is the bad of the previous age that will be destroyed. The good will be transformed into a new philosophy of goodness that will endure into the New Age.

In the Age of Pisces, women were sold as chattel, traded for gold or cows or goats. They became slaves to their husbands. Marriages were made for political gain or to ensure peace between nations. Children were betrothed to each other, sometimes as soon as they were born, to bind the alliances of their fathers. Women were forced to wear iron chastity belts to keep them "pure" while their husbands were away fighting in the Crusades in the name of the Lord. Some cultures prohibited women from owning property. And not until this very century were women granted the right to vote for their leaders in the United States, one of the most progressive countries on the planet.

Pisces was a patriarchal age, in which men held absolute dominance over women. Marriage vows contained, until very recently, the terms "man and wife," instead of a term that would even come close to granting some sense of equality and partnership. Women carried the blame for the Original Sin, because, according to the Bible, it was Eve who was first seduced by the snake in the Garden of Eden, and who then seduced Adam, getting them both banished from paradise.

In the Age of Pisces, men made the decisions and women followed. For most of the Piscean Age, women were not even given control over their own bodies.

Also, under the influence of Pisces, old religions, which revered an earthly mother goddess who bore fruit and cradled humanity in her fertile lands, were crushed under the patriarchal pressure of modern religions and their concepts of "Our Father, who art in Heaven ..." There could be no talk of a cosmic mother. Painters depicted God as a wise and aged man with a flowing beard, holy illumination glowing in His eyes.

This philosophy of masculine superiority became the justification to subjugate women, to make them second- or third-class citizens, rather than equal partners in this life. Catholics still bar women from entering the priesthood. They are permitted, at most, to become nuns, spiritual wives of Jesus Christ, subservient to the men of the cloth. The Inquisition is gone, but its suffocating sense of self-righteous control remains and women are its victims.

But God is neither man nor woman. The clumsiness of language forces us to describe this supreme being in terms of gender, but its essence extends beyond that, encompassing all. God is the union of all the energy in the universe, feminine and masculine, yin and yang.

The Age of Pisces also had its positive effect. It brought an awakening of spirituality. It brought religions based on the concepts of fraternity and compassion. It gave us works of magnificent art and majestic architecture. It gave us inventive art, creative art, sublime art. The same church that tried to so rigidly control every aspect of people's lives opened the way for the great art of the Renaissance, for Michelangelo to paint the ceiling of the Sistine Chapel.

The religions of the Piscean Age also promoted great acts of charity. Priests worked among lepers when no one else would. Mother Teresa today still works among the starving and sickly poor of India.

And now, as we step into the Age of Aquarius, the good principles of all religions will be preserved and expanded upon in this golden age of spirituality. The beautiful and profound messages of the past will bloom in the new conscience of humanity. Women will take their place beside men as equals; discrimination, whether because of race or social class, will be eliminated.

But the challenge for religions to adapt to the changes in people, to recognize that the meanings of the holy books are open to all of us, will crush some of the world's most powerful churches and force them all to change forever.

According to Nostradamus, the Catholic papacy itself will not survive the transition. One reason could be what he described in a letter to his son, César, at the opening of his now-famous collection of prophecies. In the letter, Nostradamus wrote that "the time comes for the removal of ignorance," an obvious reference to the New Millennium, which Nostradamus referred to as a golden age of peace that would last two thousand years.

Although a devout Catholic himself, Nostradamus's prophecies do not bode well for the Vatican. In his letter to Henry II of France on June 27, 1558, Nostradamus wrote that the "great Vicar of the Cope [the Pope] shall be put back to his pristine state; but, desolated and abandoned by all, will return to the sanctuary destroyed by Paganism, when the Old and New Testament will be thrust out and burnt."

Nostradamus is not the only prophet to foresee the collapse of the papacy. St. Malachy's predictions about the succession of popes from 1143 to the present have proven correct, even though he died in 1148. Born Maelmhaedhoc O'Morgair in 1094, Malachy became Archbishop of Armagh in 1132. In his prophecies, Malachy used a descriptive phrase to refer to each pope, evoking something about the coming pope's name, his family background or coat of arms, or about an aspect of the pope's period as head of the church. Pope Pius XI, for example, was indicated by the name *Fides Intrepida*, meaning unshaken faith. Seeing as how he spoke out against both Hitler and Mussolini and denounced Communism, the name certainly fits. John Paul II, the former Archbishop of Krakow, was born on the day of a solar eclipse and once worked in a quarry in Poland. Malachy refers to him as *de Labore Solis*, or the worker of the Sun.

Malachy's prophecies were supposed to extend from 1143 to "the end of the world." And, according to them, there are but two popes remaining. Malachy called the last "Petrus Romanus," or Peter of Rome, and said he "will feed his flock among many tribulations; after which the seven-hilled city will be destroyed and the Judge will judge the people."

Further evidence of the coming collapse of the Catholic Church is also believed to have been foretold by no less than the Virgin of Fatima. Three children ranging in age from seven to ten first saw the apparition of the Virgin Mary on May 13,

1917, outside the village of Fatima, about eighty miles north of Lisbon. The Lady told the children not to be afraid and to return on the same day for the next six months. Word spread quickly, and by the time of her third appearance, five thousand attended. On that visit, the Virgin said that World War I would soon end, but that "another, more terrible" war was to come during the reign of Pope Pius XI and would be preceded by a strange light in the sky. Pius XI did not even take office until five years after the prophecy, and it wasn't until more than twenty years later that the meaning of the strange light was known.

On January 25, 1938, the sky over the northern hemisphere was filled with a strange crimson light. *The New York Times* dedicated almost a full page to coverage of the event. World War II, of course, erupted the following year, just shortly after the death of Pius XI.

This third prophecy was kept hidden until 1942. The children refused to reveal what they had been told, but one of them forwarded it to the Vatican, where it was kept secret. Even now, only the part concerning the war has been released, despite the Lady's instruction that it should be fully disclosed in 1960. There is reason to believe that the remainder deals with the destruction of the Church somewhere around the year 2000. On October 15, 1963, a German newspaper printed what it said was the text of the prophecy: "For the Church too, the time of its greatest trial will come. Cardinals will oppose cardinals and bishops against bishops. Satan will march in their midst and there will be great changes in Rome. What is rotten will fall, never to rise again. The church will be darkened and the world will shake with terror."

It may be accurate. In 1909, before the Virgin spoke to the three children, Pope Pius X foresaw the destruction of the Church in a vision. He fell into a semitrance during an audience with the General Chapter of the Franciscans, his head slumping onto his chest for several minutes. When he opened his eyes, there was a look of horror on his face.

"What I have seen was terrible," he said. "Will it be myself? Will it be my successor? What is certain is that the pope will quit Rome, and in fleeing from the Vatican he will have to walk over the dead bodies of his priests. Do not tell anyone while I am alive."

That there are terrible times ahead for the Vatican seems clearly foretold. But all religions will be forced to change or perish now that the "time comes for the removal of ignorance," as Nostradamus wrote. Aquarius is the age of wisdom, in which we no longer accept matters simply as articles of faith; the age of freedom, when we refuse to allow religious dictates that fly in the face of reason to shackle us.

There are indications that this is already happening. In the small South Florida neighborhood of Biscayne Park, the Reverend David R. Simpson led two hundred members of his congregation to quit the Episcopal Church and join a national network of charismatic congregations in February 1996.

It was just one example of a growing trend in the United States, especially among the generation known as baby boomers, the same generation whose numbers fed the antiwar movement of the 1960s. More and more American Protestants are breaking from their traditional denominations to join with others of similar mind in movements described as evangelical, charismatic, fundamentalist, or liberal. It appears, church scholars say, that many among this generation find that they have less in common with another Baptist or Presbyterian than they have with someone of another religion who shares similar views.

The disaffection that led to what Simpson described as his rebellion, and that leads many more to seek a church outside of the more common groupings, comes at a time when several of those traditional church denominations are grappling with profound questions of doctrine within their walls. At the time of Simpson's defection, for example, the Episcopal Church was still considering whether or not to ordain homosexuals. Others are debating the place of women within the church hierarchy. The Church of England has been torn by the question of whether a belief in reincarnation is acceptable or not.

That major religions would be facing such challenges to their basic structures and doctrines is reflective of the increasing energy of the New Age affecting their flocks. The New Millennium opens an era of renewed and individual spirituality, in which we will no longer seek interpretations of the scriptures from others, but will connect directly with the universal spirit and understand the meaning of the holy works for ourselves.

But we must first pass through the final days of the dying era, which, as all eras before it, will burst forth in a concentration of negative energy, some of which we are already witnessing.

In the Book of Revelation, the Bible speaks in apocalyptic terms of blood, pestilence, suffering, and violence—all the horrors to be rained down on humanity before the chosen stand beside God in the millennium of peace that reigns thereafter. Many interpret this to mean the end of the world. But it is not the end of the world, it is the end of the past. These are not contradictory concepts. In the symbolism of the Bible's verses, the world as we know it comes to an end and all humanity unites in peace to bring the way of Christ to all the Earth, to bring the spirit of Christianity out of the Book and into our lives. This is the very spirit of the New Age, of compassion and caring for our fellows on Earth, of fraternity and unity and peace. But before it comes, the old must be purged. The only way it will be purged is through a washing away of the sins of the past and the thinking of the past, to open the way for what is to be. And as many devout believers in scripture say, those times already are upon us.

As the millennium comes to a close, as we inch toward the New Millennium, they will be magnified. The meeting of millennia is always a time of upheaval, but even more so now. Now, the impact of the moment is multiplied, because this is the meeting of two thousand years of history with the year 2000—two times two. Pluto, the planet associated with crime and death, has entered Sagittarius, and will remain there as we cross into the next millennium. The negative power of Uranus, its destructive rebelliousness, induces people to band together to destroy rather than to build; to impose upon rather than to tolerate. Is it any wonder that crime seems to be raging beyond control in our streets? That terrible acts of terrorism threaten our daily lives? The season of the storm is upon us. The painful cosmic birth brings perversions of the mind, perversions in our thinking.

In the Bible it is also written that before the final Judgment, the Antichrist shall walk among us, leading us against God. He already is. But there is not just one, there are many. The word "Christ" comes to us from the Greek *Christos,* a translation of the Hebrew *mashiah,* meaning messiah, or one who is anointed. Today, Christians think of Christ as the only one, the only Son of God. The Antichrist is the one seen as leading us against the teachings of God. But the word itself is a derivative of the term meaning *anyone* who is anointed. In that sense, the Antichrist is anyone who works against the ways of God, against the ways of humanity, leading us against the values of peace and tolerance and compassion that Jesus Christ espoused. And there are many here right now who are trying to do just that.

In the last few years there has been an explosion of sick social formations, of Doomsday cults, of militant separatist and racist groups. One of the most recent and glaring examples is the Japanese cult Aum Shinrikyo, which translates to Aum Supreme Truth. The sect began as a yoga school in 1987, founded by a charismatic mystic named Shoko Asahara. In Asahara's dark vision, a final apocalypse is imminent, maybe as soon as 1997, and government efforts to eliminate his movement will coincide with the beginning of the end of the world. That apocalypse, according to the cult's teachings, would leave behind Aum's enlightened followers and a tenth of everyone else—a mistaken belief yet quite a convenient one for Asahara to spread in his effort to attract disciples.

Asahara is now suspected of masterminding the March 20, 1995, nerve gas attack on three Tokyo subway lines that killed ten and sickened thousands more. Eyewitness accounts show it to be a painstakingly planned assault. A man wearing big sunglasses, brown pants, and a surgical mask stepped aboard a subway car carrying a foot-long rectangular object wrapped in newspapers. The surgical mask drew no undue attention in the midst of the Japanese hay fever season, but as soon as the man sat down, he started fingering the package he had brought with him. At the next stop, he stepped off, leaving the package. Within eleven minutes a pool of oily water spread on the floor, people's eyes and heads began to hurt, and the gas was claiming its first victim, an elderly man seated next to it. People panicked and ran. Within thirty minutes the same thing happened at five other stops. Doctors identified the chemical as the nerve gas sarin, used by Nazis to dispose of victims in the concentration camps of World War II.

When police raided the Aum's headquarters after the attack, they found fifty cult members in tiny cubicles, all suffering from malnutrition. Most swore that they were fasting voluntarily. Six had to be hospitalized. Police also found tons of toxic chemicals, including some used to make sarin.

Asahara went into hiding, but he released two radio messages. In one he said, "Disciples, the time to awaken and help me is upon you. Let's carry out the salvation plan and face death without regrets."

Asahara and his followers are hardly the first, or the only, Doomsday cult to preach apocalyptic messages of death. In 1978, the Reverend Jim Jones, founder of the People's Temple, led more than nine hundred of his followers in a mass suicide. Jones thought himself the reincarnation of both Jesus Christ and Vladimir Ilyich Lenin and had visions of an impending nuclear holocaust. On the day of the mass suicide, Jones ordered his cult members to drink from a tub of Kool-Aid laced with cyanide and tranquilizers, then he put a bullet through his head.

Currently, the Order of the Solar Temple exists as an international apocalyptic cult. It had claimed sixty-nine victims by the start of 1996. The group first came to be known on October 5, 1994, when fifty-three people died in simultaneous suicide-murders in chalets in Switzerland and Canada. The group's two leaders, Luc Jouret and Joseph di Mambro, died along with the others, leaving behind a letter that was delivered posthumously. In it they wrote that they were "leaving this earth to find a new dimension of truth and absolution, far from the hypocrisies of this world."

Autopsies revealed that some of the victims had as many as eight bullet wounds to the head. Investigators looking into the deaths also found five properties belonging to the cult. Two—an apartment outside Montreux, Switzerland, and a villa near Avignon, France—had been set to explode in a blast of fire.

Then on December 23, 1995, police in the French Alps found the burned bodies of sixteen cult members arranged in a star formation, with their feet toward the ashes of the fire.

The investigation of the cult had begun before the two mass suicide-murders. Allegations included reports that the cult's leaders were involved in money laundering and gunrunning. Specifically, Jouret and di Mambro were alleged to have pur-

chased military equipment in Australia and resold it in the
Third World.

Australian authorities said they found no evidence of the
gunrunning, but they did discover that the two cult leaders
repeatedly visited the country between the mid-1980s and their
deaths. Jouret told acquaintances that he had been drawn to the
country by the "mystic appeal" of Ayers Rock, the huge mono-
lith sacred to the Aborigines, and even asked if he could hold a
religious service there. The Aborigines said no.

Eighty-six people died on April 19, 1993, at the Branch
Davidian compound outside Waco, Texas. Their charismatic
leader, David Koresh, believed himself to be the anointed
"lamb" entrusted to open the Seven Seals of the Book of
Revelation and set loose the apocalyptic sequence leading to
Judgment Day, the end of the world and, with it, the downfall
of Babylon. To Koresh and his followers inside the Mount
Carmel compound, outsiders, or noncult members, were
known as Babylonians. When federal agents came to close in
on the cult for alleged weapons violations, the heavily armed
Branch Davidians held them off for fifty-one days, before
dying in a blazing fireball that engulfed the compound as the
agents charged in. It was the fiery apocalypse Koresh had
promised to bring forth rather than allowing himself to be
taken.

But Koresh also described himself as a patriot and his followers as an umbrella group of far right and heavily armed
"militias" who feared a government conspiracy to take their
rights away and impose a single world government. Such
groups extend throughout the United States and often espouse
white supremacist philosophies. They are little more than
American versions of the neo-Nazi groups gaining widespread
membership across Europe, targeting Jews and various non-

white or non-Aryan people as enemies and active participants in the conspiracy.

The neo-Nazis in Germany alone are believed responsible for thousands of hate crimes against minorities—arsons, murders, and beatings. They are blamed for 1,500 attacks in a single year, 1994. But the relatively quiet militias sprang into international notoriety on April 19, 1995, the second anniversary of the assault on Waco, when a car bomb exploded outside the Alfred P. Murrah building in Oklahoma City with such force that it ripped half of the 9-story structure away and killed 169 people, 16 of them children. Those accused in the bombing included 2 members of the Michigan Militia who were outraged by the Waco incident.

All of these groups, along with all of those who promote violence and death as a means of purging what they see as evil, are the armies of the Antichrist. The philosophies of the groups based in hate, the groups that choose death over life, are counter to the ideals of the New Millennium. They are the final beatings of the wings of the dying era.

In the oldest teachings of Indian philosophy, this was the era of Kali Yuga, the age of taking from you to give to me. Each of the Yuga span millions of years, so it is impossible to say when exactly one might begin or end; but by looking at the characteristics of the time we live in, we can tell that we have passed through the extended reign of the Kali Yuga and are now reaching the end of our crossing. Some years still remain, but Kali Yuga was the era of the worst wars, destructions, and impositions of monarchies—of "I command and you must follow." It was the dark age of humanity, bringing the destructive cleansing of the Earth and its people to make way for the new tomorrow. Now we are entering the era of Satva Yuga, the era of wisdom, of light.

Between now and then, there will be many more prophets of doom, suicide cults, and neo-Nazis trying to rescue ideas that don't work. And this is as it should be. We live in times of crises; we live in apocalyptic times. In God's infinite wisdom, we are being shown all the ugliness of the dying era so that we may see how we do not wish to be, to prepare us for the next giant step in the advancement of humanity. Pisces was an era of lessons for all of us. It gave us both the chance to choose and to learn by our choices. We could hear the message of Christ and choose to follow the path of righteousness and goodness, or we could choose the path of greed and intolerance and see the damage they do. It has been a long and painful journey through Pisces, filled with many difficult lessons. Many innocents have suffered. But by bringing out all the vile intolerance, by bringing out the false prophets who would choose death over life, we hasten the change to the new way of thinking where racism, bigotry, chauvinism, greed, and hate will be rejected. We hasten the change to the time when life, our own and that of others, will be revered, for what more precious gift have we been given than that of life itself?

The Bible mentions a thousand-year-long peace that follows these times of trouble, heralded by the Rapture, as it is described in the Book of Revelation. Many interpret this to be a physical event, in which thousands upon thousands of the faithful suddenly disappear, carried away to live in heaven. But the Bible is filled with symbolism, and I think of the Rapture as an awakening, an enlightenment of the mind and spirit. The more who witness the evil done by groups founded on hate or founded on dark visions of Doomsday, the more will reject them. They will "awaken," "see the light," recognize them for what they are and turn away, turn to goodness. Turning away from hate, we turn to love; turning away from separatist doctrines, we turn to fraternity; turning away from racism, we turn to humanity and compassion; turning away from death, we turn to life and a respect for all life. Turning to all of these things, we adopt the philosophy of the New Age. Thus, the divine plan is completed: the more who witness the cults of hate, the more who will reject them, and the sooner we step into the glowing glory of the new era. The lesson of the Age of Pisces is learned and we are ready to begin a new life in peace and harmony.

But the Book of Revelation also speaks of widespread devastation, of earthquakes and floods to come in the time of the Apocalypse. That time too lies just ahead, between now and the time of peace.

# 5

## Changes in the Heavens, Cleansing on Earth

In the final years of this millennium and the first of the new, the Earth itself will be rocked by the most powerful celestial forces known in the recorded history of humanity. There will be earthquakes, volcanic eruptions, and cataclysmic flooding. Climatic changes will bring drought and famine.

Then the heavens themselves will rain fire in the form of comet and meteor showers.

These are the times of trouble and terror foretold by Nostradamus, predicted by the stars, and envisioned by true seers from the Incas to Edgar Cayce. The Bible's Apocalypse approaches, but it is not the end of the world.

As horrible as it sounds, this is but the time of transition, the time of cleansing, and we will come through it changed, but ready for the new era. Look at what we have seen already in what have been the great disasters of our day: on October 17, 1989, an earthquake of 7.1 magnitude on the Richter scale tore through San Francisco as the third game of the World Series was about to start, collapsing buildings and a section of the San Francisco–Oakland Bay Bridge, crushing cars, and sparking raging gas fires that consumed whole buildings in the city's marina district. It was terrible. Yet the final death toll, which many expected in the early moments of the quake's aftermath to reach into the hundreds, if not higher, was only sixty-two.

When Hurricane Andrew, one of the three most powerful hurricanes of the century, came tearing like a horrible scythe through South Florida on August 24, 1992, carving a swath of destruction from the shore to the Everglades in which whole neighborhoods full of houses were torn down to their foundations, it was terrible. The storm caused an estimated $25 billion in damages, the most destruction of any natural disaster in U.S. history, left 250,000 people homeless, and sent insurance companies plummeting into bankruptcy in its wake. Yet tearing as it did through a county with nearly 2 million inhabitants, the storm accounted for only 15 deaths in South Florida.

And again, in Japan, on January 17, 1995, when an earthquake registering 7.2 on the Richter scale slammed the port city of Kobe, collapsing what were previously thought to be earthquakeproof buildings and highways, crushing neighborhoods and, again, sparking horrible fires that burned through the city for days, it was terrible. Many observers predicted that the damage to the port would cause irreparable damage to Japan's economy as shipments of goods and food were blocked for months, at least. And there was fear that—with the roads and port devastated—hundreds or more would die in the aftermath from lack of food, water, and medical attention. The final death toll was close to 5,000, a horribly large number, but perhaps not so large when you consider that Kobe held nearly 1.5 million residents.

The loss of any life, to be sure, is a cause for sadness. But with the possibility—no, the probability—that in each of the above cases the mortality would go much higher, if for no other reason than because of the massive concentrations of potential victims, the results are stunning. And illuminating. Because although the upheavals ahead will match or surpass any of these examples, the goodness of the cosmos will not allow its children on Earth to perish en masse. Most of us, the *vast* majority, will survive and emerge with new concepts of how to live and make our place on our planet.

What comes is the wiping clean of the slate, the clearing of the way for the new, brought on by powerful planetary forces aligning to exert tremendous force on the Earth and its magnetic field.

The correlation between planetary conjunctions, the alignment of two or more celestial bodies, and earthly disasters have been recognized since ancient times. An astrologer at the court of Nineveh, more than twenty-six hundred years ago, wrote that "When Mars approaches Jupiter, there will be great devastation in the land."

The Babylonian priest Berossus, as quoted in Stephen Skinner's *Millennium Prophecies,* wrote: "All terrestrial things will be consumed when the planets ... shall all coincide in the sign of Cancer, and so be placed that a straight line could pass directly through all their orbs. But the inundation will take place when the same conjunction of the planets shall occur in Capricorn."

Have the times that they spoke of come and gone? Were they disasters on what we would now think of as a small scale, although devastating in the tiny cradle of civilization that then existed? Alignments of planets similar to the ones they both spoke of have been seen time and again since their words were known. And it is likely that priests and seers in those times would be best served by delivering prophecies that would come to pass in the short term, which their masters could see and be awed by. But the point these ancient prophecies show is that the impact of the planets on the Earth has been known for thousands of years, at least. And that knowledge has not been limited to priests and prophets of ancient times.

Sir Isaac Newton built on the work of his contemporary Johannes Kepler in the area of "true astrology," trying to turn astrological prediction into a useful and practical scientific tool. Through his studies, Newton found ways to accurately predict not only weather patterns, but also earthquakes and other natural occurrences. As a vivid example of his ability, Newton forecast a rare sequence of natural events in England culminating in destructive earthquakes and storms—to occur twenty-three years after his death.

Newton calculated that at the time of a certain solar eclipse the Moon would be at its closest to Earth, at what is known as perigee, and Jupiter would be close enough to trigger powerful seismic and atmospheric conditions. Newton stated that the sequence of disturbances would begin with the rare appearance of the Aurora Borealis in the first three months of 1750. As predicted, the Northern Lights flickered mysteriously over England—followed by deadly storms packing 100-mph winds and a series of earthquakes that devastated London.

Despite his incredible forecasting ability, little is known of Newton's methods of prediction. But other scientists have set to studying the correlation between planetary conjunctions and natural phenomena. Several have found evidence supporting the theory that solar eclipses and planetary conjunctions working together trigger powerful upheavals in the Earth's crust.

According to this theory, as a total solar eclipse passes over a region, it seems to stretch some invisible line of force, drawing it taut like a violin string. Later, when the planets align in certain conjunctions at specific angles to or near the same point of the Earth, the force they exert seems to snap the line of tension, triggering an earthquake.

Evidence supporting the theory can be found in the undersea earthquake that set off massive tsunamis that pounded Chile's shore in May 1960. Just seven months earlier, on October 2, 1959, a total solar eclipse passed over Concepción, Chile. At the time of the eclipse, Mercury and Mars were within 1 degree of each other, Saturn was exactly 90 degrees from the eclipse, and Uranus was 90 degrees from the Sun and Moon.

On May 22, 1960, Mars passed a point in exact 180-degree opposition to the 1959 eclipse. The first quake was felt the day before, as Mars inched near that point, but the shock on May 22 was the most violent ever felt up to that time, since the advent of official records in 1881. It was so powerful that the description given of it at the 1961 world's earthquake conference in Helsinki said the "shock was so severe that the whole body of the planet, down to its core, rang like a bell."

The quake set off a series of murderous tidal waves all the way across the Pacific Ocean, destroying Waikiki Beach and devastating the entire city of Hilo, Hawaii. Four giant waves were followed by one of the worst tropical cyclones in Hawaii's history.

Similar eclipses and conjunctions preceded some of the worst natural disasters, and were predicted in advance, almost three quarters of a century before the great quake of 1960.

In 1885, examining the position of the Moon, Dr. A. J. Pearce predicted that on the day following the total solar eclipse of August 29, 1886, "there would be a great quake on the Italian peninsula." At 11 P.M. on August 30, the people of Naples, Italy, were thrown from their beds by the most severe earthquake to rock the region in twenty-nine years.

At the time of his initial prediction, Pearce also noted the coming conjunction of Mars and Jupiter on June 27, 1886, and said the position of the planets indicated "severe earth shocks near the 78th degree of West Longitude may, therefore, be expected ..."

On August 31, 1886, two days after the eclipse, at 9:51 P.M., an earthquake left forty thousand people homeless in Charleston, South Carolina, which sits almost exactly at 80 degrees west longitude, incredibly near the point predicted by Pearce. A meteor shower swept through the sky overhead just before the massive earthquake, although few thought anything of it at the time. But on September 5, the city was hit by another severe shock, followed by a large meteor trailing a long tail of fire. On October 22, about fifty meteors fell over Charleston again, again as the ruined city was shaken by a violent tremor.

Three years earlier, almost to the day, a conjunction of Mars and the Moon crossed the point that had been held by Jupiter during a total solar eclipse a few months earlier. Almost immediately the greatest volcanic eruption of modern times exploded with such a roar that it was heard three thousand miles away.

The eclipse passed over the area on May 6, 1883. The Moon was at perigee just before the eclipse, and Jupiter was at 90 degrees celestial longitude. Three and a half months later, on August 27, Mars and the Moon crossed the same celestial longitude previously occupied by Jupiter during the eclipse. As they did, Krakatoa blasted four and a half cubic miles of itself into the upper reaches of the atmosphere. Three fourths of the island disappeared. Giant waves one hundred feet tall raced into the South China Sea and the Indian and Pacific oceans, coming ashore as far as eight thousand miles away. Three towns on neighboring Java and everyone in them were wiped completely from the face of the Earth. Thirty-five thousand people died immediately. For thousands of miles around the blast site, the volcanic dust spewed into the atmosphere, completely blocking out the Sun—turning day to pitch-black night—for two weeks.

The last total eclipse of this millennium happens on August 11, 1999, cutting a southeasterly path from the North Atlantic to China. The central point of the eclipse's path will move across southern England, northern Europe, and Turkey along the way. Exactly one week later, on August 18, the planets align in an extremely unusual formation known as the Grand Cross.

Looking to the heavens at exactly 12:01 A.M. on this date reveals the Sun, Mercury, and Venus gathered in Leo, the Lion; Jupiter and Saturn in Taurus, the Bull; Uranus and Neptune in Aquarius, the Water Bearer; and the Moon and Mars in Scorpio, with Pluto nearby in Sagittarius. The clusters of planets thus will reside exactly across the zodiac from one another—Leo across from Aquarius, Taurus across from Scorpio—to form the four points of a celestial cross. The formation itself, with so many planets entering powerful aspects of each other, is likely to trigger tremendous lines of force, especially in the areas touched directly by the passing eclipse. But the Grand Cross also foretells widespread upheaval symbolically. In various forms of astrology, Scorpio represents not only the Scorpion, but also the Eagle, the sign of wisdom as well as death. The symbolism of the Grand Cross then becomes obvious—in the images of the Lion, the Eagle, the Bull, and the man—auguring the apocalyptic prognostications of the Bible.

St. John described them clearly in Revelation 4:7: "And the first beast [was] like a lion, and the second beast like a calf, and the third beast had a face as a man, and the fourth beast [was] like a flying eagle."

The signs of the Grand Cross also represent the four heads of the cherubim in Ezekiel, and the four symbols on the last card of a tarot deck, the world.

The significance of the alignment is unmistakable and unde-niable, but scientists also provide another reason why the move-ments of the planets will spark a period of droughts and famines, foretold in the Bible and foreseen by Nostradamus.

Sunspots are areas of lower temperature, which cause them to appear as black spots against the rest of the Sun's surface. They have been observed in China since A.D. 188, but it wasn't until 1843 when Samuel Schwabe discovered their periodic pattern of activity. For reasons yet to be fully explained, increases and declines in sunspot activity correspond almost exactly with Jupiter's twelve-year orbit around the Sun. For more than sixty years, meteorologists have recognized that periods of maximum and minimum sunspot activity both coincide with periods of extreme weather on Earth. An increase in sunspot activity causes a heavily ionized solar wind, bombarding us with an increase in every kind of solar energy, from visible light and radio waves to ultraviolet and X rays, which in turn causes severe weather on Earth, producing both abnormally high amounts of rainfall and severe droughts.

Recognizing the pattern of sunspots and droughts, scientists successfully predicted the severe drought and heat that affected England in 1975–1976—more than a quarter century before it happened. Using the same cycle, severe drought is expected again around 1998, with exceptionally powerful weather patterns developing in 1999 as the sunspot activity shrinks to a minimum.

Other scientists have also noted a long-term sunspot cycle of particularly strong activity occurring every 179 years. Both 1778 and 1957, 179 years later, set records for sunspot activity. Both years also happened to coincide exactly with the extremely rare three-way conjunction of Jupiter, Saturn, and Uranus. But an even more rare alignment of the planets comes just as we enter the New Millennium.

On May 5, 2000, this extremely unusual alignment of the planets promises to put phenomenal pressures on the Earth. Writers sometimes mistakenly refer to this formation as the Grand Cross, but in fact what occurs is not a cross at all. Instead, on this day the majority of the planets, including massive Jupiter and Saturn, gather in opposition to the Earth. The only exceptions are the outer planets. Neptune and Uranus sit together at 90 degrees from the Earth in Aquarius, and Pluto remains in Sagittarius near our home planet.

The effect of this alignment on sunspot activity can only be imagined. But the gravitational influence alone is so over-whelmingly stacked against the Earth that the pull of the planets could easily set off the complete reversal of the world's magnetic field predicted by Edgar Cayce.

Cayce foretold of a shift in the Earth's axis around the year 2000 that would spark disastrous flooding of coastal regions. The quickly rising floodwaters would sweep over northern Europe, bury southern England under the sea, and cause Greenland to disappear, he said.

I include his vision here because it fits so remarkably with what the stars foreshadow: the path of destruction he describes matches almost perfectly the path of the last solar eclipse of the millennium.

There is evidence that the Earth's poles have switched places before. Geologists sampling the ocean floor around the mid-ocean ridges have found the record of the reversals maintained in molten rock that has cooled at different times. As the rock cools and solidifies, it retains a weak magnetic field, matching the polarity of the Earth's field at the time. So far, geologists have counted at least twenty instances when the Earth's magnetic poles have been transposed, each seriously impacting life on the planet.

This record of reversals could more easily account for discrepancies in the evidence discovered from the Ice Age. Popular theory has it that the great glaciers crept slowly across the continents. But that can't possibly account for the massive mammoths and other animals found trapped in blocks of solid ice—caught so suddenly that they are found still standing, with undigested food in their stomachs. Only a sudden switch in climate would explain how these great beasts were frozen so quickly that their meat is still edible when they are discovered.

The last time the planets formed conjunctions similar to what we will see on May 5, 2000, was nearly thirteen thousand years ago. If they then exerted the same forces that we can anticipate this time around, the timing would coincide with the approximate date Cayce gave for the final devastating series of cataclysms that sank the lost continent of Atlantis and set off the Great Flood of Noah's time described in the Bible and repeated in nearly every culture around the world.

Just before the thousand years of peace that are to follow, the Bible says similar events shall come to pass. In Mark 13:8, Jesus tells St. Mark that the signs of his return will be when "nation shall rise against nation: and there shall be earthquakes in divers places, and there shall be famines and troubles: these [are] the beginnings of sorrows."

But Jesus also tells Mark "be ye not troubled; for [such things] must needs be, but the end [shall] not [be] yet."

The Bible, of course, is not the only place where predictions of natural disasters are to be found. Nostradamus, one of the most stunningly accurate and precise prophets ever to live, foresaw a series of cataclysmic occurrences coming, he wrote, in "the year 1999, seventh month," preceding a golden era of two thousand years of peace. By Nostradamus's way of calculating the seventh month is actually September, because the great prophet marked the start of each year—the first month—in March.

Significantly, in March of 1999, Pluto will be slipping again to its normal celestial position as the outermost planet. What we think of as the ninth planet in the solar system actually has been occupying the place of the eighth since 1979. It is a rare, cyclical occurrence, but once every 248 years, Pluto actually moves inside Neptune's orbit, closer to the Sun than the eighth outermost planet, for a period of 20 years. The impact of this transposition of Pluto and Neptune has yet to be precisely determined (since Pluto itself wasn't even discovered until 1930), but as Pluto returned to its more common place in the solar system two cycles previously, in 1503, Nostradamus was born in St.-Rémy-de-Provence, France.

Around the time Pluto exits Neptune's orbit in 1999, Nostradamus predicts widespread famines and drought, as well as vast inundations that will cover entire land masses. That the destruction and flooding will follow the path of the last solar eclipse of the millennium is indicated in Century IX:31, where Nostradamus writes, "The trembling of the earth at Mortara, the tin island of St. George half sunk ..." The reference to the island of St. George clearly indicates England, where the umbral shadow of the 1999 eclipse will pass over Plymouth south of London. The same shadow will cover almost all of Italy on its course to the southeast, including Mortara. Nostradamus's reference to an "abundance of fire and fiery missiles [that] shall fall from the heavens" could indicate comet and meteor showers bombarding the Earth, which are also predicted by the calendar of the Incas and by a noted Russian scientist, Dr. Immanuel Velikovsky.

In Velikovsky's first book, *Worlds in Collision*, published in 1950, he examined the accounts of cataclysmic natural phenomena retained in the records of the major ancient civilizations, including such diverse peoples as the Greeks, Samoans, Native Americans, Chinese, Egyptians, and Hebrews. All contained references to a stopping of the rotation of the Earth, all similar to what is described in Joshua 10:13: "So the sun stood still in the midst of heaven, and hasted not to go down about a whole day."

A similar description is given in Habakkuk 3:11, where it is written that "The Sun [and] the Moon stood still in their habitation ..."

An extremely long night is recorded by peoples on the other side of the world. Velikovsky concluded that this was the result of a massive comet that passed so close to the Earth sometime between 1502 and 1450 B.C. that it temporarily slowed Earth's rotation. As it passed, he wrote, the comet's tail twice struck the Earth, causing earthquakes and major changes in the geography of the world.

Ancient calendars provide strong support for this theory. Ancient Hindu Aryans marked a calendar year as 360 days long. So did the Babylonians, the Egyptians, the Chinese, the Incans, and the Mayas. So many diverse cultures, all with extraordinarily accurate astronomical and astrological capabilities, all computing the year as 360 days long. The Mayas, for example, calculated the period of the Moon at 29.5209 days—as accurately as we calculate it today using computers. Why, then, would all of these cultures discard their accuracy in calculating the calendar year? Or, to put it another way, why would so many dissimilar cultures around the world all have made the same mistake in calculating the length of their years, all at about the same time?

The answer may come in the writings of Plutarch and on a stone tablet found near Tanis in 1866. Plutarch wrote that in the times of Romulus, one of the founding brothers of the ancient city of Rome, the year was in fact 360 days long. The Egyptian tablet recounts that the priests of Canopus ordered the addition of five days to the calendar around 237 B.C. "to harmonize the calendar according to the present arrangement of the world."

Egyptian mythology even gives an explanation for the addition of the 5 days, as it describes the birth of the 5 primary gods of that ancient culture. The Sun god Ra gave birth to Shu and Tefnut, the twin gods of time. They, in turn, gave birth to Geb (Earth) and Nut (Sky). Nut also appears to have been the spouse of Ra, who was outraged when she began cohabitating with her brother and ordered that she could not bear a child in any of the 360 days of his year. To help her, Thoth, the god of science and mathematics, bet the Moon and won $\frac{1}{72}$ of her light, which he grouped together into 5 new days. These he added to the year, thus allowing Nut to give birth to Osiris, Horus, Set, Isis, and Nephthys. Five days is exactly $\frac{1}{72}$ of 360.

Others theorize that an asteroid or planetoid actually struck the Earth somewhere in the distant past, with results similar to what Velikovsky suggests happened. This may have been what caused the final devastation of Atlantis, sending the continent to the bottom of the ocean.

For an idea of the force even a minor meteorite or comet packs when it races through the atmosphere and slams into the Earth, we need only look back to the summer of 1908. To this day, no one knows quite for sure what body of disruption set off the explosion that leveled trees for hundreds of square miles and wiped out an entire herd of reindeer in a remote area of Siberia near the Tunguska River. Evidence exists in ample enough quantities to know that *either* a comet or a meteor weighing some 100,000 to several million tons blazed brilliantly as it rocketed through the sky at a speed of about twenty miles per second on that June 30. The friction of the atmosphere could have superheated a comet composed primarily of frozen matter as it rushed in, setting off the massive explosion that knocked a man out of his chair at a trading post fifty miles away. But the large quantities of iridium discovered at the site—rare in earthly soil—suggest a meteor that somehow exploded before it hit the ground, thus leaving no crater. Whichever, it exploded with the force of a large hydrogen bomb.

One farmer, more than 125 miles from the blast site, described how he watched the fir trees bend completely over as they were hit by the hurricane-force winds spreading out on the front edge of the blast's shock wave. He said he had to latch on to his plow with both hands to avoid both being carried off by the wind wave, and witnessed how "the hurricane drove a wall of water up the Angora [River]."

Calculations made after scientists reached the center of the blast site indicate that the object that came rushing through the atmosphere that day could have been a rock about 250 feet across or a lump of iron a mere 80 feet across.

But what came past our planet in blazing fury in the distant past appears to have been much, much larger—gigantic, in fact, by comparison.

Velikovsky concluded that the massive comet that threatened the very existence of life on the Earth went on to be trapped by the Sun's gravitational pull, to exist now as the planet we know as Venus. His theory led Velikovsky to predict that Venus would have an atmosphere filled with concentrations of hydrocarbons, that the Moon would be strongly magnetic, and that Jupiter would send out strong radio transmissions. All of those predictions have now been confirmed.

Support for Velikovsky's theory can be found in the myths and writings of various ancient cultures. The Jewish Talmud describes the comet's tail as "fire hanging down from the planet Venus." Greek mythology gives the account of Phaeton, who took the fiery Sun across the sky in his father's golden chariot, burning mountains, reducing cities to burnt ruins, and filling the air with smoky ash before he was stopped by Zeus.

The Aztecs called Venus Quetzalcoatl, the "feathered serpent," and wrote that at one time, the "sun refused to show itself and during four days the world was deprived of light. Then a great star appeared; it was given the name Quetzalcoatl ..." Its appearance came at a time of widespread famine and pestilence that left many people dead.

The current Incan calendar ends in 2013. The Incan scholar Willaru Huayta states that at that time a huge asteroid will pass so close to the Earth that it will disrupt the world's gravitational field and orbit, setting off a series of calamitous natural disasters from tidal waves to earthquakes and volcanic eruptions. The force of suddenly slowing the Earth's spin would be more than enough to spark every one of the Incan predictions—the world would shudder and its rotation would stall as the comet effectively slammed on the brakes, but the momentum of their motion would keep the oceans and mantle crust of the planet spinning at close to full speed. Tectonic plates would shift and slide, causing mammoth earthquakes, and cavernous rifts would open to spew molten lava. The force of the ocean would bring giant tidal waves crashing against the slower moving land masses and totally cover entire regions.

But even the Incas agree that this will not cause the end of the world. Instead, they say, people will emerge from these catastrophes as a new "sixth generation." Many other esotericists also make reference to a "sixth subrace" being born in the Americas whose members will be possessed of powers of perception reaching far beyond the limited dimensions of reality most of us allow ourselves to perceive.

And despite the dire gloom of many of his predictions, even Nostradamus wrote to Henry II that this would not be the end because "by my ... prophecies, the course of time runs much further on."

What follows, of course, is the golden age of peace foreseen by Nostradamus and foretold by the stars, coming in the New Millennium.

# 6

# The New Dawn

Aquarius is the age of discovery, the time to touch our innermost being, and to reach out into the most distant depths of the universe. As we travel further into ourselves, farther into space, and further into the New Millennium, our discoveries will lead us to change everything about ourselves and our societies.

People will no longer be interested in the sea or the Earth in the way they were in the Age of Pisces, as territory to be conquered and owned. In the Age of Aquarius, we go inside to discover our inner selves, our inner values, our inner spirituality, and the matter of dealing with who we are, what we are, and why. We have been overly concerned with what lies outside of us, with the material things we can have, following the dictates of others without truly examining their value for ourselves. Now is the time for us each to step back from the external and tune into the internal. This does not mean that we will all suddenly adopt the life of Indian mystics, shun all material goods, and seal ourselves off from all worldly things ascetically. Aquarius is the time for integration. We will hold the things of value, the things we personally find to have value, and let go of the rest. We will not look for others to determine what is of value for us, either in material or spiritual things. Madison Avenue does not make us want anything; we make ourselves want it. But up until now, we tend to value things we are told are of value, told *to* value—the most luxurious car rather than the most practical; the fashions we saw the models wearing rather than the clothes we like and feel comfortable in. Today, fashion is the mechanism used by those trying to make money by exploiting our insecurities. In the New Millennium, we will judge things for ourselves. We will dress as colorfully or as simply as we like. No one will decide for us. We can thank the advertisers for showing us the options, but the decision will be ours. Our capacity to do so comes with our spiritual rebirth, our philosophical rebirth, our intellectual rebirth.

Our concept of beauty changes as we step further into the New Age. Beauty exists in everything; it is up to each of us to find it. There is beauty in a rain shower and in a rainbow, beauty in dawn and in night, beauty in the sky and in the muck at our feet. We become our own beholders, free of the judgments and dictates of others. Everything in nature is beautiful. The fury of a hurricane or a tornado is terrifying and terrible in its destructive force yet beautiful and awe inspiring at the same time. A savage animal crouched over a fresh kill is beautiful and horrible at once. In that terrible killing, in that death, is the essence of life. And it is beautiful.

In India, they construct horrible, yet beautiful, temples for the dead, known as the temples of silence, because whoever enters there is never to speak of what they have seen. The living who enter must face backward, in such a way as to not see what is there, so as to never tell. The followers of Zoroaster, the Farsi, take their cadavers wrapped in white cloth to these temples and lay them on the roof for the vultures to eat. It is a horrible sight, the vultures eating the flesh of the dead, but beautiful too once you realize it is done so that the flesh does not go to waste. If it can be eaten by worms in the ground, then why not by the birds? Once the vultures pick the bones clean, the faithful pour acid over the skeletons and the calcium runs down the sides of the temple, washing the walls in white. It is horrifying, seeing the enormous birds with hunks of thighs and legs in their beaks. It is horrifying to know what ghastly paint makes the walls of the temples shine brilliantly in the sunlight. But it is life and death together, and it is at the same time both horrifying and beautiful.

In the Age of Aquarius, nothing human will horrify you. Nothing human will intimidate or frighten you. Nothing human will paralyze you. In the Age of Aquarius, people open themselves to everything that is life. We learn from everything. Seeing the tiny ant at work, you will say, "How efficient," or "How dedicated." We can learn from the way the ants work in concert for the common good, from how they communicate. It awakens something inside us to learn something new. People with closed minds or those who think they know everything allow nothing new to enter. In the beginner's mind, everything is new and everything is possible. We must enter the New Millennium with a beginner's mind, open to all the possibilities, open to learning.

The New Age is not an outdated, old-knowledge, old-wisdom age. It is an age of openness—to new life and new knowledge. Nature and the universe and everything in it teaches a lesson, if only we could open ourselves to it. And it is not only in the things of animals and trees and the sky. Everything holds a lesson, including the things of humans. The works of Shakespeare are just as beautiful, just as much a part of the natural order as the things of the jungle. We can learn from it all, from everything, learn what to hold true in our hearts and what to reject. That is the grand lesson of the Age of Aquarius: knowing truth and true value.

As time goes on and we drift ever deeper into the flow of the astral current of Aquarius, enjoying more of its gifts every day, the negative and the darkness distance themselves. The influence of the New Age already is upon us, but grows stronger by the day, increasing almost imperceptibly as we travel through this time of transition between the power of Pisces and the dawning of Aquarius. But it is like watching our children grow. From yesterday to today there was hardly any change, none that we would notice; but looking back we see how big they have grown and how quickly time passes. So, too, with the evolution of Aquarius and the illumination that it brings. The clouds drift away and the veils from the enclosing folds of our minds clear. The symbolic waters of life poured down upon us by the Water Bearer, Aquarius, loose us from the chains that for centuries have bound us. Aquarius as a sign colors the New Millennium, bringing with it a new way of thinking for a new society—collective individualism.

The more we know about ourselves, the more we know about those around us. Everyone and everything is a unique entity in the universe, yet all hold the same spark of life; the same cosmic breath blows life into all of them. In that similarity, to know one is to know all. The closer we come to knowing the spark of life, the very depths of our spirit, the further that voyage into our innermost selves takes us and the closer we come to our fellow humans. The Aquarian principles of individuality and humanity go hand in hand. As we become increasingly in tune with the spirit of the New Age and go deeper inside ourselves to touch our innermost feelings to find our innermost values, it is as if our skin becomes more sensitive, our very being becomes more sensitive to everything and everyone around us. An injustice to anyone or anything hurts the same as a wound to our own flesh. We feel the pain of any who suffer, whether they live in Africa, or Bosnia, or in our own home. We begin to feel the pain of all humanity and, naturally, wish to end it. No one wishes to live in pain. We all do whatever is necessary to end it, whether it is physical, emotional, or spiritual pain. If the pain of our brothers and sisters in the great fraternity of humanity feels as our own, we will wish to end their pain so that we may end our own. Helping others is helping ourselves. In the increasing sensitivity of the coming age, we finally adopt the reality of Christ's message, finding compassion for those around us, doing unto others as we would have them do unto us.

This is the age of true love for all humanity, of true fraternal love between all beings. It won't happen all at once, of course. We won't, as I've said before, wake up one morning and suddenly go rushing door to door giving our neighbors kisses on the cheeks. But with each passing day, we will act—must act—a little differently. One day, we stop to help a child; on another, we help that child's family. One day, we stop thinking of others as different because of their color or their creed, and soon enough we find that they too have stopped thinking that way as well.

None of this is forced. Force is contrary to the Aquarian way. There is no more imposition of will. Not on others, and not on ourselves. In the Aquarian Age we enter the flow of nature, we float with the current, and that takes us naturally to the Aquarian ideals. As the spirit of the New Age flows over us, it saturates us, our souls, and our thinking. There is no need to do anything more than to open ourselves to it.

In part, the voyage of discovery takes us back in time. The generations of today already are touching the engrams of the past, buried deep in their minds. These engrams, these sums of our ancestors' learning and our own learning through a thousand generations, remind us of how we had to work together once just to survive. As people pushed into the wilderness of the New World, barn raisings were common communal events. All the neighbors gathered on a given day, carrying their tools, and together pitched in to put up a barn. What might have taken one or two people weeks or months to accomplish was done in a single day. In ancient tribes, we banded together to ward off the fierce animals that came to attack in the night. We joined together in the hunt to bring down a beast that was too ferocious for any lone hunter and large enough to feed all. To stand by and watch any individual be hurt or killed was to weaken ourselves, in numbers and in strength. If the numbers of our tribe diminished, we as individuals were weakened. Eventually, our day would come too, with too few left to fend off the animals in the night.

This sense of common purpose is being born again, even as you read this. And it is a way of thinking that each of us carries within us. The engrams now being awakened by movements of the planets are not just the ancestral teachings buried in our DNA. They are our own memories as we come to realize more and more in the New Millennium.

More than half the world believes in reincarnation, but the modern Western religions do not. It's understandable. Reincarnation threatens the hold the power seekers within the Church have over us. How can we be threatened with everlasting damnation, with being doomed to dance on the hot brimstone coals of hell, if death itself is not everlasting and, in fact, our souls reincarnate? Their power is based on fear, specifically on the fear that we shall burn forever in hell if we sin and do not repent our sins in *this* life. If we can atone for the sins of this life in the next one, the fear is lessened and the whole basis of their power is shaken. In the Eastern religions, we pay for the sins of the last life in this one; if we improve, we have a better life next time and, eventually, are freed from the cycle of reincarnation and join with the universal spirit when we realize that our soul and the Buddha soul are one.

But the process of reincarnation is neither a license to sin nor a debt to carry and be punished for until we purify ourselves. Karma is not about punishment, it is about learning.

Reincarnation is a chance to improve ourselves and our world, a series of lessons leading to the realization that we share the spark of universal life. We are all part of the great cosmic consciousness. Why, then, would we be sent here with but one chance to prove our worthiness before we are cast eternally into hell? Is, then, a native in the wilds of Africa who lives and dies without ever hearing the teachings of Christ, but who does not sin in the Christian sense, cast into hell or accepted in the Kingdom of Heaven? Why would God put that African here in the first place if he or she cannot ever read the Bible and gain admittance to the heavenly realm?

It is said that when we are born, an angel touches a finger to our lips and tells us not to tell what we know. That is why we are born with a cleft in our lips and no remembrance of what we have lived before. But those who are spiritual enough can. They have not distanced themselves from the universal spirit and through it are able to connect to their pasts.

Edgar Cayce, variously known as the sleeping prophet and the miracle man of Virginia Beach, quite accidentally discovered his own capacity for "hypnotic clairvoyance" through a friend. Cayce, a simple farmer's son with a profound belief in the Bible and Christianity, suddenly caught laryngitis when he was twenty-one and lost his voice for a full year. He went to several doctors, but none was able to help. Desperate, Cayce accepted the help of a local man with some ability in hypnosis. While in a trance, Cayce not only described his ailment, but also described the treatment that would cure him.

Soon enough, Cayce discovered he could use his newfound talent to diagnose and help others. He wound up giving some thirty thousand "readings" in all, about 80 percent of them to seek cures for ill and infirm people, whether near or at a distance, achieving miraculous results in the vast majority of cases and never accepting payment for his help. Every word Cayce spoke under hypnosis was recorded by a stenographer, and the accuracy of Cayce's readings was confirmed again and again by the actual subjects. The same records also exist of Cayce's non-medical readings.

After nearly twenty years of helping others with his medical readings, Cayce was asked by a curious friend if his clairvoyance could shed light on more profound questions of life and philosophy. Cayce had never been troubled by such questions. He accepted without question what he read in the Bible. Still, he eventually agreed to allow himself, under hypnotic suggestion, to see if he could give the man's horoscope.

In his usual trance, Cayce delivered a short horoscope. Then, without being asked, without it ever being suggested that he look deeper, Cayce ended his reading with the stunning words, "He was once a monk."

The idea that people's spirits returned to the earthly plane, that we in fact reincarnate in lifetime after lifetime, had never crossed Cayce's mind. In fact, to his religious way of thinking—Cayce read the Bible through from beginning to end at least once a year from the time he was ten—the very concept was sacrilegious. Still, as time went on he allowed the matter to be probed deeper as he lay in his hypnotic trance. Yes, he explained in various readings, astrology contained some truth, although it was not yet refined enough to take reincarnation into account, nor did its practitioners fully understand the effect of the planets on people's glandular systems.

Slowly, Cayce became convinced that these new discoveries about reincarnation did not conflict with his religious views. Through long discussion and soul searching, he came to accept that our reincarnations are a series of learning experiences, phases we go through until we achieve spiritual perfection.

Although much more difficult to prove than the medical readings, evidence for these "life readings," as he came to call them, turned up in historical records and in the accuracy of statements that the conscious Cayce had no knowledge of. In the case of one man, Cayce told him he had been a soldier in the Confederate army during the Civil War, even giving his name at the time and where he had lived. The man searched out the archives and found the name of the twenty-one-year-old man who enlisted as a color-bearer in 1862. Another time, Cayce, lacking formal education, made a reference during a reading to Jean Poquelin, whose mother died when he was young. Cayce had no idea that Poquelin was the real name of the French dramatist Molière, whose mother died when he was a child. Cayce didn't even know who Molière was, much less Poquelin, until after the reading.

Under hypnosis, Cayce explained that we all carry the memory of all of our past lives and experiences buried deep within our minds. Reaching them, remembering them, Cayce said, required us to go through a sort of trapdoor into the deepest reaches of our minds.

It is said that to know of what has gone before, we should ask a child. Children have not closed their minds to the possibilities. They have not sealed Cayce's trapdoor. Newborns understand everything we mean in the way that angels are said to: they understand emotions. It is not the word "no" that makes a child cry; it is the feeling that rushes in with it—the anger or disapproval or fear. It is not the words of the lullaby that soothe; it is the feeling of overwhelming and unconditional love that comes with it. As words allow children to express themselves in more detail, they also seal children off from that universal language, increasingly putting limits on what is to be expressed or repressed. Children's talk of things seen in their sleep is dismissed by adults as nothing but a dream, rarely welcomed as a possible vision; the things seen while awake are dismissed as the products of an overactive imagination. So slowly but surely, the children adopt the ways of the adults and seal themselves off from the past.

In the New Millennium we all are allowed to remember again. We all will realize that we are touched by the divine spark of life and that it flows through us eternally. We come, we learn, we come again. We evolve. It's like the trees. In the winter, the trees appear to die. Then, in spring, they flower again. What is in the archetype of nature is in the human soul and in everything. We return here again and again until we have learned and no longer have to return. Then we return if we choose to. The power of choosing comes when you know what is behind you. When you have tasted all the wines, you choose the best one. The older souls among us have returned to help guide us into the New Age, to help us learn what they have learned. They will teach us to reach back to our previous lives so that we can remember what we have learned for ourselves. They will teach us to connect to the great cosmic spirit of life that surrounds everything in the universe.

In his hypnotic state, Cayce described a similar universal tapestry in which was recorded every event, every motion, every sound—everything—that occurred in all of the cosmos since the beginning of time. Again, remember that Cayce was not a very educated man; he only went to a simple country school through the ninth grade. But, in trances, he spoke of what he called the "*Akashic* records." He explained that *Akashic* is a Sanskrit word referring to the fundamental spiritual composition of the universe. Sometimes he referred to the records as "The Universal Memory of Nature," or "The Book of Life." He said we each have the ability to tap into this field of energy and read from it, if we can tune our sensors to a high enough degree of sensitivity. Whether we can read it or not, we each project our every thought and action onto it.

Hollywood producers speak of an interesting phenomenon. For months, they say, they won't receive a single "western" movie script in the mail. Then, suddenly, they are inundated with them. Or, suddenly, it seems everyone is writing suspense thrillers with a computer as the culprit. It's as if, one producer said, someone had tapped into the collective unconscious, scratched the universal fabric; that someone somewhere thought of something and suddenly every writer at a typewriter, word processor, computer, or scratching out their ideas in longhand felt the thought, had the same inspiration. But that is exactly what happens. A butterfly flapping its wings in the Amazon *does* set off a snowstorm in Montana. We, and everything in the universe, are all connected. Every action has a reaction. Every thought is connected to the universal spirit, and every one of us is both a transmitter and receiver connected to it, if we learn to be. Our thoughts are tiny electrical impulses leaping across the synaptic junctions of our brains. That much we know. Every thought, then, travels across a gap, a space, to connect to the next junction. What science hasn't discovered yet is that no matter how minute those impulses seem to our measurement techniques, to our scientific instruments, they are strong enough to connect to the universal current flowing around us. And all of us, whether we recognize them as such or not, receive impulses from that universal current. We are all connected to the flow of energy pulsing through everything. Those sensitive enough, in tune enough, can recognize it. But since science can't yet measure that universal current, scientists don't accept its existence. Only that which can be measured and proven with scientific methodology is real in the scientific world.

Now comes the realization that things exist even though we have not been able to prove their existence. What lies ahead is a total explosion of the human conscience and a total restructuring of science. Like the Phoenix rising from the ashes, we will rebuild anew, keeping what is good and discarding what is bad or useless. In the New Age we break free of centuries of false doctrines, destructive indoctrinations, absurd ideas, and children's stories about God, religion, education, medicine, and love. The corrupt foundations of false society crumble. This time of crises is not the signal of the end of the world. What comes is not the end, but the beginning. The dream humanity has lived for centuries ends and we awaken to a bright new day, a bright new way.

Now, in the Age of Aquarius, everything becomes unified. All of our differences, all of our dualities mix together like the fragrances of a flower shop, with all of the different flowers adding their bouquet to the overall mix until they are inseparable. Each individual flower remains distinct and individual, each one's fragrance is unique and discernible when you come up close to it, yet joined together in unity with the others in the wonderful mixture that is the smell of the shop.

Our individual worth comes from inside, from what we have inside, through our development, our evolution, and what we can give to society. Now our drastic differences dissolve and we integrate into the greater whole. We integrate and unify with those around us and unify with the energy of the universe, with the great cosmic spirit.

Mystically, Aquarius signifies friendship. Friendship is a sacred word in the New Millennium. Friendship bursts upon us in its most elevated sense, in its most noble aspect—with understanding, collaboration, and fraternity. Love and friendship will have nothing to do with possessing or ego. The idea of love meaning "you belong to me" ends in the New Age. The thought of friends of convenience, friendship based on an ulterior motive such as business, ends. Love and friendship based on anything other than pure love, the divine and pure love of God, changes the sentiment into a coin of exchange—you no longer have love or friendship because of who you are, but because of what you do or can do for me.

This is the era of peace, of unity, of love. The polarity of Aquarius, Leo, floods us with its complementary characteristics. The celestial throne of the Sun, Leo, encourages, ennobles, enriches, and enlightens us for the growth of our hearts, the growth of our inner beings. Together with Aquarius, Leo promotes the integration of our individuality with our unity with all humanity. We realize that we must first be something in and of ourselves to be something for others.

Under their combined influence, friendship with an agenda disappears into true fraternity, into pure unity. Then we can prepare ourselves for unity with the universal spirit.

Aquarius also reigns over originality. The era brings a burst of originality in the arts and in ourselves. Everything from music to painting feels the energy of the age and expands into fresh frontiers of expression. In some ways, this can already be seen. Whether you like rap music or not, you must admit it is a totally new form of artistic expression for the downtrodden poor, a total rupture from the music of the majority. Reggae too suddenly reached out through the airwaves and into our consciousness with a totally distinctive and previously unknown form. Painters as well, with their tactile form, were also able to tune in earlier than most others. Perhaps it was because they felt the influence of Aquarius earlier, felt the revolutionary forces of evolution when modern art went through such dramatic changes so many decades in advance of the New Millennium, giving us the unmistakably rebellious form of painting called abstract expressionism.

In the Age of Aquarius, we break from the past to invent the future we desire in our society and in our person. The answers we find will be wholly new ones, totally original ones, but they require a thorough examination of what has been and what we wish to come.

All of our institutions as we know them must adapt to this new reality. The time is not just for the integration of humanity, but for the integration of all its codes, canons, and concepts. We are not just reinventing ourselves, but all of our systems of society. The rules that bind, the laws that chain, the edicts that keep us in constant conflict with ourselves, all come crashing down.

The Bible speaks of the Second Coming of Christ, of a millennium of peace that comes when Jesus returns anew and all of us join together universally. The time is at hand. Christ is coming, but not physically, spiritually. The Bible spoke in many metaphors. The Spirit of Christ is what comes now in our souls, in our awakened spirituality. The cosmic inner Christ is coming. It is time to realize that we are all the "children of God," and that the "Son of God" came to show us the way to unite with that divine universal spirit.

It is Christ's message now that is awakened and becomes a reality. We do unto others and have compassion for all. Now is the time to put Christ's message and Buddha's message of love into practice, to take them from the level of mere words and turn them into action. Too many people make a show of going to church. They go not seeking, but to be seen. They go to church, but the Church does not go in them. They make an act of presence, repeating rituals mechanically, without feeling, failing to grasp the meaning. Or they go begging. Ungrateful for what they have, wishing it were more, they go asking for more. That is not the way, nor the purpose, of religion. Aquarius is an age of gratefulness. We must get up every morning thankful for yet another day of light, of love, of opportunities and possibilities. The affirmation of every day should be, "I feel good. I feel loved by nature, by the wind, by the universe and everything in it."

What is important now is to seek the true meaning of the messages of the masters. For two thousand years, those messages have been exploited, used by preachers, pastors, and priests to build gleaming castles, to build treasure troves of riches while the poor starved. They served as salesmen of paradise and perdition to build palaces. But few put the message of the masters, the message of love, into practice. Often, it was just the opposite. Too many have been killed in the name of God. The Crusades sent army after army to wage war in the Holy Land. Inquisitors and pious prosecutors sent too many so-called heretics and witches to their deaths. Now we must renounce all the venom of the past, release the centuries of anger, and breathe the peace and love of the Age of Aquarius. We must stop being beggars seeking salvation or praying for prosperity and become grateful participants in the order of the universe, in harmony with it.

That means loving all of nature, loving each other, loving ourselves. In the Age of Pisces, religion taught us that our bodies were impure. In the left-and-right, black-and-white, good-and-bad thinking of that age, we divided our bodies into top and bottom. Everything below the waist was evil and foul; above, goodness. We had to cleanse our bodies to purify our souls. In extreme cases, this gave rise to the customs of wearing hair shirts to mortify the flesh and of self-flagellation, whipping our own bodies to expunge the evil of the flesh. Naturally, then, in that way of thinking, sex had to be bad. But what is more natural? Enjoying sex does not inherently have to be bad. Enjoying the pleasure of passion is not necessarily evil. Wanton abandon, seeking partner after partner to fill an emptiness in our souls or using sex as a means of power over others is wrong. But our flesh alone is neither good nor bad; what we choose to do with it is. In the Age of Aquarius, we seek unions based on true inner love; within them, we share of ourselves without restraint, enjoy each other without guilt.

The concept of guilt itself comes from the Age of Pisces. Power seekers and power holders used it as a means of control, to keep us in check, to keep us from being truly free. Their wanting us to obey their rules and guilt was a way of making sure that we did. In the New Age, we will no longer fall prey to guilt. Guilt gets its strength from our letting others decide our truths for us. It only has power over us if we let others have power over us, if we depend on them for our values. Guilt is an admission that others are setting the rules of our behavior. But it is also an admission that we have not yet accepted ourselves as our own guides. It is an admission that we cannot decide for ourselves what is right and what is wrong, that we are only trying to avoid doing what someone has decided is wrong. Once we realize the truth for ourselves, we will lose our doubt and no one will make us feel guilty.

In the New Age, each must follow the path dictated by his or her own heart. We will *know* what is right, and knowing this, we will not permit others to draw us into their conceptions of right and wrong.

The thought of us deciding for ourselves what is correct, what is right and what is wrong, will dramatically affect the hold our institutions have over us. It forces change in our religions, our laws, and our governments.

We all know society has grown sick, that our values have collapsed. Our politicians rather than seriously tackling the problems and working on cures try to profit from the disease. They spout streams of speeches, torrents of words about the ills, the crime, the needs, but only as a means to get themselves elected or reelected. Too many are merely purveyors of propaganda, with the message changing as often as suits their needs.

We have been victims of propaganda, of all kinds. When countries become enemies, they try to convince their peoples that the people themselves are enemies. As governments go to war, they paint each other's people as evil and ugly. Always, the mask painted on the enemy is horrible, exaggerated. When the governments become friends, the masks are repainted. Now that we seem to be at war with ourselves, the masks are painted on all of those who are different, depending on where the propaganda is being delivered. If you are poor, it is the rich who are to blame; for the rich, the poor are at fault; for those of any given race, it is those of the others who come to destroy their lives. When we see things for ourselves, we will no longer accept the images of propaganda. Not of others, nor of ourselves. No one else is to blame for our problems. Society itself is seeking to heal itself, and simple propaganda is not even a momentary palliative. As we go inside ourselves and our differences disappear, we will seek to cure ourselves, and those who try to use ignorance and ill will to turn us against each other will find themselves increasingly isolated.

We will turn a deaf ear to those who work against the spirit of unity and fraternity and back only those who work toward it. Politicians who support the causes of humanity and unity will gain our support. Through them, our governments too will change or perish. Laws aimed at imposing anyone's will on another, at dominating others, will be eliminated. The whole of our courts, our system of laws and judges and attorneys, comes crashing down.

What comes now is a true democracy, a democracy of the self, in which we are all the owners of the Earth and the rulers of it. It is anarchy, in a way, but not anarchy as we think of it in Piscean terms, in which small groups tried to destroy government so that they could impose their will on others. This is a new anarchy—positive anarchy. It is anarchy in keeping with Christ's message, founded in fraternity and compassion, a humane anarchy. In it, the poorest person, the most primitive native will reign as ruler of his or her own universe. From within each of us, from the recognition of our place in the universal order will come the right to rule and the reasoning to rule— justly, pacifically. It is the anarchy of light and love.

With it comes a bonding of humanity and a union of science and spirituality that will change forever the way we think and live.

# 7

# New Powers of Nature, New Powers of the Mind

There are those who say that when Atlantis, Lemuria, and other continents sank in ancient times, at least some of their inhabitants escaped to other planets with all of their knowledge and discoveries. Now, as what has been structured—the continent of concepts, ideas, and beliefs—sinks, people around the world will escape within themselves, journey to their inner selves, to discover and know what is real. In the New Millennium, humanity seeks the wisdom of the elders, of the ancestors, of the primitives, and of the natives. As the restrictions of the era of Pisces fall away, we become free to experiment, try, and learn what is useful and eternal. The coming age opens the door to a time of great scientific expansion and humanitarian deeds. The moment the millennia meet is a portal in time, a passageway that leads to the greatest discoveries of human history.

Science and spirituality join hands after centuries of fighting. We tear away the veil of deception and hypocrisy to make way for the flowering of a new springtime for humanity. We will discover tremendous new powers in nature, and tremendous powers in our minds.

What until now have been tentative trials in the field of holistic medicine become realities. Illness, disease—all manners of sickness begin in the soul and grow to the mind before showing their symptoms in the body. Everything we know as a physical illness is of the last stage of a process of disintegration that begins with disharmony. Think of those infected with the HIV virus and how they have prolonged their period of normal health, staved off the deadly effects of AIDS through exercise and a positive outlook. Stress and worry, we know, weaken the immune system. Yet rather than attacking the cause, we take vitamins to supplement our systems. Cancer victims have literally reversed the progress of their disease, cured themselves through healthy lifestyles that include healthy attitudes. People at peace with themselves and their world, happy people, are much more likely to be healthy people.

In the New Millennium we will know that even the tiniest cell in our bodies communicates its needs to us; each listens to the vibrations of our spirits and our minds; each, in its own way, has its own mind that registers every one of our thoughts, the good and the bad. We know of the power of psychosomatic illnesses; why shouldn't there be psychosomatic cures? Now comes the medicine from within, by learning to listen to our own bodies and getting our bodies to listen to us. We can put the world of DNA at our service, cooperating with us, once we learn to cooperate with it. If you program your cells with constant thoughts of "I don't feel well, I'm sick, I'm sick, I'm sick," the cells hear it so much that they *will* get sick.

The moment has arrived to paralyze the negative mind—the acquisitive, comparative, fatalistic mind—and let our hearts guide us. With positive affirmations we can break through our programming and cure ourselves. Let the positive power of the Age of Aquarius flow through you to nurture and heal you, and through you, the Earth. In return, the planet will open its plenty to us again, to share the secrets of yet to be discovered curative plants and herbs that will improve our lives and strengthen and heal our bodies.

The ancients and the primitives knew the power of the plants and herbs. They knew the power of the Earth. For every ill on Earth, there is a cure that comes from the Earth. It is merely up to us to find them. Watch the animals. When an animal feels ill, it eats certain herbs or grass. It seeks the cure for what ails it in the Earth. Animals listen to their bodies and know that the remedy is in the Earth if they can only find it.

In the New Millennium, the Age of Aquarius, our union with each other and with ourselves also brings us into union with our great Mother Earth. Aquarius signifies a return to nature. In the Age of Pisces, humans whipped and destroyed Mother Earth, ignoring the hazards and the harm they did as they laid down asphalt and cement, let smoke belch forth from factories, poured chemicals into once-pure rivers and streams, spewed gases from motors, and threatened the very air we breathe. Mother Earth is severely wounded, and now comes the time to heal our mother, who has given us of her plenty and asked for nothing in return. Spiritually and philosophically motivated people have battled to stop the destruction for decades in so-called green movements. Now, scientists too are putting their seal on the warnings of those green revolutionaries. Scientists have documented the weakening of the ozone layer and the threat of global warming. Scientists and environmentalists both have joined together to make us all realize the reality that we must protect and expand the rain forests, must cover the Earth with a carpet of green vegetation again, because these are the lungs of the world.

This revitalization of nature, this rebirth of the Earth begins with each of us, each on our small piece of ground, each in our own lives. We each must cultivate and care for our own small plot of land, even if it is but a window box outside a New York apartment.

This Earth belongs to us, as long as we are in this incarnation, and the world is the world as we want it to be. We are each a tiny universe unto ourselves, connected to the cosmos. If you, in your universe, are at peace, you contribute to the overall peace. If you begin individually with peace and love, that drop of peace and love falls in the lake that surrounds it, sending out ripples to touch the farthest reaches. You will have an effect on the entire planet, on everything in the universe, beginning with yourself. Do not think that because you are just one humble person, one poor person, one poorly educated person, that you cannot contribute to the beautification of the new world. Each of us who opens themselves, who learns to listen and understand the message of the great cosmic order, will receive what amounts to a mandate to reach out to the Earth in an all new way, to touch the Earth in an all new way. Hearing that message, scientists will show us how to make deserts bloom, to make barren lands fertile, to cleanse the air we breathe.

Already, the spirit of the New Millennium calls to us to join in the effort. Communities and cities have banded together in massive recycling efforts, trying to reuse or find new uses for what once was waste. This is only the beginning. We are on the verge of a total transformation of this terrestrial globe. There remains much of this Earth that still lies virtually unknown to us. In those hidden places lie treasures that the Earth has held for us to discover. As we do, we also will discover all new ways to use our planet. We need to learn to listen to and heed our great mother, the Earth.

We need to take our lessons from nature. Somehow, because we walk upright and use our intellects, we came to consider ourselves totally separate from the animals, instead of merely different from them. Yet the animals have many lessons for us. The

strongest animals do not eat meat. Mighty elephants, the largest
animals to walk on this planet, eat leaves and grains. They live
to a great old age on this simple diet. Animals of tremendous
strength—horses and cows—live on diets of pure grasses and
grains. The animals with short lives eat meat. Tigers and lions,
fierce and powerful as they are, live but a few short decades.

We too need to listen to our bodies as the animals do. And
we will learn to, to know what we should eat and how we should
care for ourselves. We already can, we just choose not to. We
close our inner ears to the shouts of our body until we become
absolutely deaf to them, or until it no longer calls out to us. We
become like those people who live next to the railroad tracks or
the airport who, after a while, never hear the train or the planes.

Any doctor knows that a pregnant woman's cravings are simply her body calling for specific nourishment. The standard joke
of a woman wanting ice cream and pickles sounds disgusting,
and it is, normally. But it is nothing more than the body shouting out that it wants certain vitamins and amino acids. Why
should only pregnant women have this ability? Of course they
don't, it's just that we are taught, programmed, to eat certain
things at certain times of the day. We are taught to eat "three
square meals" every day, taught to clean our plates so that nothing goes to waste.

And then, as we grow older, we must fight a losing battle to
keep our waistlines from bulging. Small wonder. Instead of listening to our bodies, learning to listen when we want fruit and
when we don't want any more, we force ourselves to adapt to an
unnatural schedule of eating. We force ourselves to finish every
last bite, and we adapt to eating more than we need. Then we
force ourselves onto unnatural fad diets, hoping to shed all the
pounds a lifetime of bad habits has heaped upon us. That
thinking is the either/or, feast and famine mentality of the era
of Pisces. Tune in to your desires, tune in to your needs, and the

balance comes naturally. Forcing ourselves to eat then forcing ourselves to fast creates constant tension within us. It puts us at war with our own bodies. It promotes the constant cycle of dissatisfaction and discomfort that leads to disease.

Nothing that you truly enjoy will harm you. *Truly* enjoying, however, is not the same as becoming addicted. The first time you smoke a cigarette and inhale the smoke down into your lungs, the body automatically responds by setting off wracks of coughing, warning you to reject the smoke. The body forces you to expel the smoke, yet, almost as soon, the first rush of nicotine narcotizes the brain and sets off a drug-induced feeling of dizziness or acceleration. The body has shouted its warning but as you return again and again to the smoke, the body quells the coughing—because the brain orders it to so that it can continue to get its pleasure.

Similarly, our bodies rarely crave sugar beyond the natural sugar in fruits and other foods. But we allow ourselves to become addicted to sugar, to pastries, sweets, and candies. And once we are addicted, we cannot hear our bodies anymore. The sugar triggers responses in our brains, not in our bodies. And our brains then block the messages our bodies are shouting out. You hear it still, upon occasion, when you look in the mirror and think, "Ugh, I should lose some weight," or when you are short of breath climbing the stairs. But you push the thought away just as quickly, you silence your body's message in favor of your brain's desire. Your brain is imposing its will on your body, instead of being in tune with it. Listen! Hear! Act upon what you know to be true before you push the thought away!

Knowledge is power. As we gain increasing knowledge about ourselves, we gain increasing power over ourselves. With it, we can even halt the hands of time. Aging begins in our minds with the thought that we only have so many years in this life to begin with. We may or may not think of an exact date or number of years, but the thought that we will not live beyond a certain length of time because that is what everyone lives to is the same thing. "On average," we think, "men and women live to be ..." And that's that. In the same manner, we think that at a certain age this will happen or that will happen. We think that after thirty, or forty, or fifty, or whenever, we will no longer be able to do this or that or the other thing. But that is the same as starting to run a race thinking that you will lose. You will. Athletes, coaches, and psychologists call it visualization. Visualize what will happen, and it will. If you think, "I can't run that far," then your lungs will burn like fire, you'll gasp for air, and your legs will wobble and give out. Think of yourself running free and easy like a gazelle in the wild, your stride steady and smooth, your breathing easy, and you *will* run farther and faster than ever before.

It's the same with aging. Someone once said, "You don't stop playing because you grow old; you grow old because you stop playing." It's true. We make ourselves old. Or we let others make us old by believing them when they say, "You shouldn't be doing that."

Remember the words from the song "Young at Heart"? Your mind never grows old unless you let it. Your mind functions until you yourself project that it no longer gives you the maximum. You have psychological immortality, mental immortality, if you want it.

When recognizing the power within ourselves, we get in tune with ourselves and become partners with our doctors in caring for ourselves. Now when we go to the hospital, we are patients, patiently waiting to be treated. We wait to be told what is wrong with us. We wait to be given a pill or a shot. We wait to be cured. In the future, we will labor with our own energy for our own cure, working hand in hand with our doctors—science and spirituality coming together.

Today, psychic and spiritual healing are considered fantastic, aberrations, or just lucky. As we go further into the New Millennium we learn to make them happen. We already can. Already the spirit of the Age of Aquarius is touching us, calling us. Hear it, and listen to it, and already these things will start to happen for you. We can learn to listen to our spirits and to our bodies. And we can learn to listen to the unplumbed depths of our minds. As we do, we will discover what today would be considered fantastically incredible powers of the mind, powers that tomorrow, in the New Age, will be considered commonplace.

Scientists estimate that we only use 10 percent of our brains. The truth is, that is all we allow ourselves to use. Out of laziness—because we don't need the rest for most of our mundane daily activities—or out of training, we close ourselves off from most of our capacity. From the time we are little, we are taught to read, taught to write, taught to think in a certain way. We are taught to do it the same as everyone else. Every day, we are taught to use only enough of our brains to do what we must and ignore the rest. The imaginary playmates of children exist only in the imagination, we learn, and should be forgotten. Soon enough, they are. Logic is what's important, and anything that cannot be explained logically doesn't exist.

Our dreams, we are told, for example, are nothing more than that—dreams, hallucinations without meaning. Rational science develops elaborate explanations of how our dreams work, how we use them to sort our impressions of the day. Sigmund Freud founded the whole of modern psychology by probing the meaning of our dreams, of the symbolism of our dreams. He told us how trains going into tunnels really exist in our dreams as metaphors for sex, and so on. Which, if the converse is true, must mean that dreams of having sex with a beautiful partner really mean I want to ride a train into a tunnel.

But it seems somewhat odd that our bodies and our minds, which otherwise speak so clearly to us, would suddenly turn to elaborate metaphors for what they wish to tell us. When we have a stomachache, it rarely means that our throat is sore or we are catching a cold. A sneeze rarely means we are hungry. Why, then, would I dream of trains when I'm thinking of sex?

No, our bodies and minds do not speak in metaphors. They speak in a language that we must learn to pay attention to and learn to understand. When we sleep, we shut off the judgmental mind, the imposing mind, of Pisces. Our bodies and minds speak clearly to us, and they open the way for us to see and hear and know more than we ever have before. In our sleep, we can tap into that gigantic unused portion of our brains. We can reach deep into our ancestral minds and forward into the unknown. We can open up the tremendous powers of mind that will be commonplace in the New Millennium. Eventually, those thoughts will accompany us and speak clearly to us when we are awake, as well.

The primitives of the jungle and of ancient times had an entirely different explanation for our dreams from the one Freud has given us. To them, our subconscious opened the doors for the spirits to speak to us. Our dreams were messages from our ancestors or the gods, often visions of what was to come. They listened carefully to their dreams and learned from them. As we became more attached to material things, to the material world, we lost touch with our dreams and lost touch with the vast well of power within us. Now comes the time to awaken the past, to step into the future.

Clairvoyance, telepathy, things that seem far-fetched, even impossible, today are possible in the New Millennium. Why shouldn't they be? Already we speak of premonitions, of déjà vu, of feeling lucky, of feeling funny or creepy. We have gut feelings and get the chills, but our logical mind pushes those thoughts away. The collective values and thinking of Piscean society, which say ESP and other powers of the mind don't exist, push those thoughts away.

Every one of us has heard of cases of twins who share a simultaneous thought or of a mother overcome by a horrible feeling of dread as her child, miles away, barely dodges a car. A mother's intuition wakes her in the middle of the night and leads her to a sleeping child's room to find him or her gripped by a dangerously high fever. We know these cases to be true, yet we dismiss them.

As quoted in Johann Peter Eckermann's *Conversations with Goethe,* Goethe commented on our capacity for sharing thoughts telepathically: "One soul may have a decided influence upon another, merely by means of its silent presence ... It has often happened to me that, when I have been walking with an acquaintance, and have had a living image of something in my mind, he had at once begun to speak of that very thing ... We have all something of electrical and magnetic forces within us."

Using powers we don't understand, animals know when a storm or an earthquake is on the way. Long before the most sensitive seismograph detects the first trace of a tremor, animals hide and fish swim to the bottom of the sea. We humans, once we become properly tuned in to our inner selves and begin to recognize our own connection to the cosmos, once we recover the knowledge of ourselves and the power within each of us, will develop powers a thousand times stronger than that of the animals.

Carl Jung, the noted psychologist, once said he refused "to commit the fashionable stupidity of regarding everything I cannot explain as a fraud."

He didn't. He found remarkable correlations between people and astrology and observed remarkable firsthand incidences of paranormal phenomena.

In a lecture he gave in 1905, Jung cited the example of Emanuel Swedenborg, the mystic Swedish scientist whose visions led to the founding of an influential religious sect in the late 1700s. Swedenborg had just returned to Göteborg from a trip to England, en route to his home in Stockholm some fifty miles away. But as he visited at a friend's house on his stopover, he suddenly became very agitated and exclaimed that a fire had just broken out in Stockholm and was spreading very fast. He said that the house of one of his friends already had burned to the ground and that his own was threatened. Two hours later, Swedenborg announced that the fire had been put out, just three doors from his house. The following morning, Swedenborg described the fire in detail: how it began, how long it lasted, and how it was put out. But it wasn't until the evening of the following day that the first messenger arrived carrying news of the fire from Stockholm. And it wasn't until the morning after that that the full report of the fire and the damage it had caused arrived in Göteborg—matching Swedenborg's account of the fire exactly.

My own life is composed of visions and revelations. Ever since I was a child, I have seen the cause of illnesses or their coming. As a child I was called "Walter of Miracles" by the people of my town, because word quickly spread about the child who could see into people's pasts and futures, who knew the causes of their illnesses and the way to their cures. Because it has been that way for me since I can remember, that I could see what was and what was to be, I at first didn't realize that I was different. Like a fish in the water, I was immersed in the spiritual world from birth and had no idea that others walked on land.

One day, for example, I was sitting at my tiny desk in the small classroom of my elementary school when I saw the bell at the entrance of my school falling. I felt a great shaking of the

Earth and saw people running. I could see it clearly, but when I jumped in shock and called out for my teacher, the ground was not moving and my classmates were sitting calmly and quietly at their desks. My teacher told me it was just a bad dream, not to worry.

The next day, I was sitting at my tiny desk again, when suddenly the Earth began to tremble, then shake violently. People ran and screamed and the bell at the entrance of my school fell—just as I had seen the day before.

But why I had been given this power and what I was to use it for did not become clear until many years later. I was in my bedroom on December 18, 1975, when I awoke suddenly and realized I was completely paralyzed. I felt completely frozen. As I lay there, not knowing what to do next, I saw that my room was completely filled with an intensely bright light. Then I saw and heard an entity—the source of the light, but with no real form or features, just a being of light. It was speaking to me, but in a mystical way because I didn't hear it with my ears, but with my thoughts. It spoke to me mind to mind, heart to heart. It told me that I had been chosen to be an instrument, that it was my mission to use my powers to help guide others through this very difficult time in which we live.

Since then I have continued to receive messages, often thanks to that asexual being of light who comes to stand by my side or who comes in my dreams to take me by the hand and take me walking along a beach. As I opened myself more and more to receive those messages, my psychic antennae became better tuned, in much the same way that a swimmer who dives in the water every day finds the motions becoming smoother and more effortless with each passing day.

But just as the ability to swim is not unique to any one individual—we all can do it if we wish—so too with the powers of the mind.

Today, scientists conduct experiments in parapsychology at a number of highly regarded institutions around the world. The United States government sponsored research on psychic functioning at SRI International, originally known as the Stanford Research Institute, for almost twenty years. In 1990, the sponsorship moved to Science Applications International Corporation (SAIC), along with the former director of SRI International.

The findings of the research at both institutions, according to Professor Jessica Utts of the University of California, Davis, division of statistics, "suggest that if there is a psychic sense then it works much like our other five senses, by detecting change ... it may be that a psychic sense exists that scans the future for major change, much as our eyes scan the environment for visual change or our ears allow us to respond to sudden changes in sound." In an example of the results of experiments at SRI, two researchers in 1975 reported that two test subjects correctly described a top secret underground government facility that they had never seen or heard of before. One, in fact, was so accurate, naming codewords and workers at the facility, that the experiment set off a security investigation into how the information got out. The same subject then went on to describe a similar Soviet site in the Urals, which also was later verified.

Many of us have had the feeling that we're being watched. In an experiment at SAIC, researchers tried to determine if there was a physiological change, a measurable body change, to support the "feeling." The researchers seated their test subjects in a room with a video camera focused on them and measured their skin's electrical changes as someone in another room tried to influence the subjects by staring at their images on a monitor. The results: there was significantly greater skin reaction when the subjects were being watched compared to control periods when they were not being watched. The researchers also noted that the effect was much more pronounced when the subject and the observer were of opposite sexes.

In research on out-of-body experiences, which we also call astral projections, Charles Tart, professor emeritus of psychology at the University of California, Davis, and a consultant with SRI International, found stunning evidence of their existence. A woman who reported frequent out-of-body experiences in her life was connected to electrodes to measure her brain patterns as she slept. Tart not only was able to record a measurable and significantly different brain wave pattern during her reported out-of-body experiences, but also was able to show that she had acquired information that she could only have gotten if she were floating near the room's ceiling.

To test her, Tart put a randomly generated five-digit number on a piece of paper—without the subject seeing it—face up on a shelf some seven feet off the ground, where it could not be seen by anyone even walking around the laboratory, and hardly by a young woman lying in bed with short electrodes connected to her. In repeated attempts on different nights, the woman reported she was not able to control her movement during an out-of-body experience and had failed to detect the number. But on the one occasion on which she said she had floated to the ceiling near the paper, she got all five numbers right and in correct order!

More than forty years of scientifically controlled experiments now support the existence of extrasensory perception. The research concludes that many of us already have the talent of telepathy, the power to send and receive mental messages from and to others; of clairvoyance, the ability to know of different places and events without the help of another; and of precognition, the capacity to know of events before they happen. Tart's research even includes studies of how to improve our ability to use our "sixth sense." In the Age of Aquarius, the veil of mystery will be lifted and we will come to understand and use the whole power of our mind.

Uranus and Neptune come together in Aquarius in 1998. This is of extreme importance in unlocking the abilities of our deep, unplumbed minds. Uranus brings the spiritual energy of our inner beings bubbling up through our minds; Neptune rules the spinal canal and the mental and nervous processes. Together, they receive and magnify the illuminating, visionary energy of Aquarius. Add to this mighty meeting of planetary influence the positioning of Pluto in Sagittarius. Pluto is the planet of the unconscious; Sagittarius, as you already know, is the sign of expansion, of magnification.

Combined in this never before seen celestial union, "it shall come to pass afterward That I will pour out My spirit on all flesh; Your sons and your daughters shall prophesy, Your old men shall dream dreams, Your young men shall see visions" (Acts 2:17).

Edgar Cayce, the clairvoyant known as the miracle man of Virginia Beach, reached out with his mind in some twenty-four thousand well-documented cases to cure illnesses in people whom doctors could not help or had given up on. In thousands more of the hypnotic trances that opened the way for his amazing clairvoyance, Cayce answered questions about reincarnation, the universal spirit, and astrology. He said astrology's primary influence was glandular, that the planets were vibratory centers of energy that impacted upon humanity. Our receptors for connecting with the universal tapestry that holds the recorded history of the cosmos, he said, lie deep within our brains, and if we could reach into that region and tune our antenna well enough, we all could see and know as he did. Cayce himself foresaw this happening—as well as its import: "It is difficult to project ourselves into such a world—a world where people will see each other's faults and virtues, their weaknesses and strengths, their sickness, their misfortunes, their coming success. We will see ourselves as others see us, and we will be an entirely different race of people. How many of our vices will persist, when all of them are known to everyone?"

There is a fantastic correlation between Cayce's visions, the visions of a basically uneducated farmer's son who barely completed the ninth grade in a simple country school, and the beliefs of Eastern religions Cayce hardly knew of.

Eastern masters say our visionary power lies in our pineal gland, that it is our "third eye," the source of spiritual and prophetic energy. Now, in the New Millennium, comes the dramatic growth of this body deep within our brains, of these receiving antennas connected to the vast collective unconscious described by Jung. Tapping in to our inner well opens the way to visions, to prophecies. Our antennas will be turned on and tuned in as they never have been before. The greatest mediums of all time are being born already; people will connect with the past and help lead us into the New Age.

Humanity returns to the simple and natural on this plane, but our spirits, as our bodies sleep, can come in contact with other realities, can receive knowledge through our astral voyages. We can develop our ability to reach out with this power and gain revelations. Charged with the energy of the coming age and opening ourselves to it, we increase our capacity to abandon our bodies, to leave our bodies, to send our spirits through space to see and know distant places through time to know the future and the past, and to connect to other spirits, other consciousnesses.

Teilhard de Chardin, the Jesuit priest exiled to China for his writings relating science to theology, wrote in "A Sketch of a Personalistic Universe" that "in a concrete sense there is not matter and spirit. All that exists is matter becoming spirit. There is neither spirit nor matter in the world; the stuff of the universe is *spirit-matter*."

The evolution of the spirit-matter, he concluded, is the princi-
pal purpose of being: "Life represents the goal of a transformation of great breadth, in the course of which what we call 'matter'
turns about, furls in on itself, interiorizes the operation covering,
so far as we are concerned, the whole history of the earth. The
phenomenon of spirit is not therefore a sort of brief flash in the
night; it reveals a gradual and systematic passage from the unconscious to the conscious, and from the conscious to the self-
conscious. It is a cosmic *change of state.* This irrefutably explains the
links and also the contradictions between spirit and matter."

Mystics speak of powers of levitation, of raising the physical body with the power of the mind. Researchers have confirmed the existence of out-of-body experiences, of sending
the spirit to explore outside of the physical body. The spiritual
awakening that comes with the New Age brings not just the
integration of science and spirituality, but a balance of spiritual and physical energy.

We will see that our bodies are but the space suit our souls
wear on this terrestrial plane. Once our mission here is completed, we discard it and move on as our true selves, our spirits
and selves intact, to the next plane.

Things that we call miracles today will be understood in the
Age of Aquarius. We will know the law of nature that makes
our miracles happen, we will know why they happen, and we
won't think of them as miracles, but as blessings.

Technology already is making this possible. Computers of
today are lessening people's workloads, speeding the processing of
information and the spread of knowledge. Calculations that
would have taken years to complete by hand just a century ago can
now be completed by a computer in a matter of minutes, if not
seconds. This computational power and speed grows exponen-
tially as the calculations of the computers are directed at making
faster and better computers. A new generation of computers—

smaller, faster, and more powerful than their predecessors—appears every eighteen months. And so it should be in this age.

Aquarius, the Water Bearer, symbolically represents the pouring out of knowledge onto the Earth and all of us. Aquarius, an air sign, signifies air and all things that flow, such as electricity. It also symbolizes progressiveness, invention, and technology. Naturally, computers are the material expression of all of these Aquarian characteristics.

The Piscean Age signaled its impending death in one destructive display of force, the atomic bomb, in 1945. The following year, the first electronic computer came into being in a laboratory in New Jersey. Called ENIAC, the computer used fifteen thousand vacuum tubes to work out its calculations. Today, cheap, handheld calculators easily handle as many or even more calculations than that first massive machine. The average home or classroom computer handles millions more. Today, computers are used in almost every field, from agriculture to zoology. In the short half century since the first electronic computer cranked out its first solution to a problem, computers have become critical partners in solving the planet's problems.

Computers have changed and continue to change our lives in every way. But one of the most dramatic effects of the computer—a testament to its Aquarian spirit—is in linking people together around the world, bringing humanity together in an electronic unity that opens the way for global unity. Linked together in the vast worldwide network of computers known as the Internet, millions of people the world over are sharing their work, their thoughts, and their hopes. An estimated 27.5 million people used the Internet in 1995, and the number has doubled every year since 1990. Through it, people who just a few years earlier would have spent their lives ignorant of one another's existence are communicating regularly. As contacts grow, sensitivities grow, understanding grows, and differences dwindle. The global connection of computers is bringing us much closer to the world envisioned by the late Marshall McLuhan, in what he called the "global village." And it is bringing us much closer to the world predicted by the prophet Nostradamus, who wrote: "Pestilence is extinguished. The world becomes small. For a long time the land will be inhabited in peace. People will travel safely by air, over land, seas, and wave ..."

Computers, of course, work hand in hand with the other marvelous technology of the Aquarian Age, the laser. Fifteen short years after the ENIAC turned electrons into solutions, the first helium-neon gas laser became a reality.

Today, lasers aid in industry, construction, communications, photography, space exploration, and surgery. The Aquarian traits of humanity and technology merge in the laser, the brilliant concentration of energy for good, rather than for destruction. A laser can destroy, but in the hands of someone who knows how to use it, it is a wonderful and healing light that makes miracles possible. In communications, lasers facilitate and speed our connections to others around the world. Lasers etch the intricate arrays of circuitry on the minute microchips that make our supercomputers of today possible. In computers, lasers give access to millions of tiny bits of information on disks, opening gateways to knowledge for millions of people. By using disks instead of paper as a means to transfer information or for everyday communications, thousands if not millions of trees are saved every year. Lasers and computers together have found their way into operating rooms around the globe, saving lives that would have been lost just a few short years ago. And lasers make possible the fiber optics technology that allows crystal-clear, high-speed connections between people and computers around the world.

Without these twin technologies, we would never have been able to take even our first steps into space, the new frontier of the New Millennium.

# 8

# Angels, Aliens, and Atlantis

On their 155th day orbiting the Earth aboard the *Soyuz 7* space station in 1985, six Soviet cosmonauts reported twice seeing a band of "angels": "seven giant figures in the form of humans, but with wings and mistlike halos as in the classic depiction of angels. They appeared to be hundreds of feet tall with a wingspan as great as a jetliner."

The angels followed the spacecraft for about ten minutes, then disappeared. Twelve days later, they returned.

"We were truly overwhelmed," said cosmonaut Svetlana Savistskaya, quoted in Sophy Burnham's *The Book of Angels*. "There was a great orange light and through it we could see the figures of seven angels. They were smiling as though they shared a glorious secret."

All six of the cosmonauts were trained professionals not given to hallucinations. Savistskaya was on her second mission into space, and on it successfully became the first woman to walk in space. They were all trained observers with impeccable credentials who said they saw angels not once but twice.

If true, the meeting was a long time coming. Humans first pushed their way into space with the successful flight of the *Vostok 1*, which carried cosmonaut Yuri Gagarin in a single orbit around the globe on April 12, 1961. Three weeks later, the United States sent its first astronaut into space, on a suborbital flight. It wasn't until February 20, 1962, that astronaut John Glenn became the first American to successfully circle the Earth, completing three orbits aboard the Project Mercury craft *Friendship* 7. But as he orbited the Earth, Glenn, a decorated, record-breaking marine pilot who later became a U.S. senator, reported something strange, something no one had ever seen or suspected, as he circled through his second orbit:

"This is *Friendship Seven.* I'll try to describe what I'm in here. I am in a big mass of some very small particles that are brilliantly lit up like they're luminescent. I never saw anything like it. They're round, a little. They're coming by the capsule, and they look like little stars. A whole shower of them coming by. They swirl around the capsule and go in front of the window and they're all brilliantly lighted. They probably average maybe seven or eight feet apart, but I can see them all down below me also."

As he studied the lights, he noticed that they would go out, then relight, like fireflies.

To this day, there are theories but no explanations.

Did John Glenn have the first encounter with some unknown celestial force?

The Age of Aquarius is the age of space exploration. As we go into ourselves and unite with our planet, we also will reach for the stars. And as we go, we will have more encounters with the unknown, with both angels and aliens.

UFOs, unidentified flying objects, flying saucers, have existed as rumors and myths for hundreds of years. For every story of an alien encounter, skeptics fire back with a dozen explanations. Somehow, in an expression of supreme egocentrism, they cling to the idea that we humans are the only intelligent life inhabiting the universe. Yet even so renowned an authority as Carl Sagan has said that the mathematical probabilities against this are simply overwhelming. If but a tiny fraction of the trillions of stars in the universe host planets, and if but an infinitesimally small fraction of those planets afford conditions capable of sustaining life, and if but a minute number of those actually have life, then there are still thousands, if not millions of life-forms in the universe.

Remember that Uranus is considered the planet ruling space travel and the unusual, or unknown, and that this outer planet entered its celestial throne, Aquarius, on January 12, 1996.

Just four days later, astronomers announced the discovery of two previously unknown planets in the distant reaches of the universe with characteristics similar to Earth's. Both planets, known as 70 Virginis and 47 Ursae Majoris, have conditions capable of sustaining life, according to the astronomers, even though they are 35 light-years—210 trillion miles—from Earth.

"We see ourselves at the gateway to a new era in science," one of the discoverers, astronomer Geoffrey Marcy of San Francisco State University, is quoted in *The Miami Herald* as saying when the announcement was made. "We can compare our own nine planets to their planetary cousins in other solar systems."

Marcy and his colleague, Paul Butler of the University of California, surveyed 120 stars and completed computer analyses of 60 of them. Finding three planets out of 60 stars showed how common, in fact, these "cousins" may be. Marcy himself said, "The answer is no—planets aren't rare after all."

Pisces was the era of the sea and of conquest by sea. In it, people pushed across vast oceans to discover the New World, extending their reach to cover nearly the entire face of the planet. Aquarius is the age of discovery and of space. Aquarius signifies our departure from this planet to probe the cosmos. It signifies air because it is an air sign and, symbolically, space.

Now comes the time of intergalactic voyages, of reaching out across vast oceans of space to discover new worlds and the life on them. In Aquarius, we reach out across the galaxies and, finally, make contact with other beings.

Rumors of astronauts making contact with aliens have persisted since the dawn of space exploration. Major Gordon Cooper, one of the original Mercury astronauts, was long said to have spotted extraterrestrial spacecraft in the final orbit of his May 15, 1963, flight. Years later, in 1980, Cooper denied this in an interview, but said he had seen and chased UFOs as an air force pilot in Germany in 1951.

"Yes, several days in a row we sighted groups of metallic, saucer-shaped vehicles at great altitudes over the base," Cooper said in a March 1980 *Omni* magazine interview, "and we tried to get close to them, but they were able to change direction faster than our fighters. I do believe UFOs exist and that the truly unexplained ones are from some other technologically advanced civilization ... I think I have a pretty good idea of what everyone on this planet has and their performance capabilities, and I'm sure some of the UFOs at least are not from anywhere on Earth."

On October 21, 1978, a twenty-year-old Australian pilot on a 125-mile training flight between Melbourne and King Island suddenly began reporting to the air traffic control tower that he was being buzzed by an unidentified flying object with four intensely bright lights. Frederick Valentich was over the Bass Strait in a Cessna 182, flying solo, when he radioed in that an alien craft was chasing his small plane. The craft, he said, made repeated passes, and the increasingly frantic young pilot reported that it appeared to be closing in and that he was being engulfed by a bright light, when suddenly the radio transmissions stopped. No trace was ever found of Valentich or the Cessna 182 he was flying.

Another incident took more than a year of investigation and review by an official British panel of experts, but finally, on February 2, 1996, the answer came as clearly as any skeptic could admit: the experts were baffled by a pilot's report of a lighted wedge-shaped object zipping nearly head-on with his passenger airliner.

Captain Roger Wills and copilot Mark Stewart were approaching Manchester Airport in a British Airways 737 on January 6, 1995, when they saw the object. It rushed at them at high speed, so close, the panel's report said, that "the first offi-cer (Stewart) instinctively ducked as it went by.

"It made no attempt to deviate from its course and no sound was heard or wake felt. He felt certain that what he saw was a solid object—not a bird, balloon or kite."

Pilot Wills described the unidentified flying object as having "a number of small white lights, rather like a Christmas tree."

Thirteen months later, the Civil Aviation Authority issued its report, ruling out as unlikely the possibility that the object was a military or light aircraft or something smaller, such as a paraglider.

"Despite exhaustive investigations, the reported object remains untraced," the CAA experts concluded.

Our encounters with the otherworldly, angels or aliens, are hardly new. They stretch back to the beginnings of time. Early mention of these "others" can be found in early Sanskrit writings, which described beings who rode a column of fire into the sky. In the Book of Ezekiel is written, "And I looked, and behold a whirl-wind came out of the north, a great cloud, and a fire infolding itself, and a brightness about it, and out of the midst thereof as the color of amber, out of the midst of the fire.

"Also out of the midst thereof [came] the likeness of four living creatures. And this their appearance, they had the likeness of men ... and they sparkled like the colour of burnished brass."

And in the Second Book of Kings: "... behold, [there appeared] a chariot of fire, and horses of fire ... and Elijah went up by a whirlwind into heaven."

Now as we push our way into those same heavens, we push our way closer to meetings on neutral territory, or on their home planet instead of ours. In the New Millennium we explode the myths of visitors from elsewhere and convert them to realities.

As fantastic as that sounds to the skeptic of today, it simply must be so, even using the logical arguments the doubters level against everything they don't believe. It defies the imagination, as Sagan said, that in a universe so vast that we cannot find its boundaries, filled with thousands of galaxies that dwarf our own Milky Way, that there would not be other life as intelligent as or more intelligent than we. Any Las Vegas oddsmaker would know which way to bet; any underwriter studying these probabilities would know the outcome. It's simply a matter of time before the contact is made. But there again, it had to be this time, the dawn of the New Age.

Aquarius not only draws us into space on intergalactic voyages, it draws us into unity. This means that in this age we not only come to know of the existence of other life not of this Earth, but we embrace it. Universal unity means just that—not just unity with the universal spirit, but a union with everything in it. As we touch the stars and other planets, we will touch the beings on those other planets. And, in the spirit of friendship and peace that permeates the whole of the New Age, we will form peaceful, intergalactic unions with them. This is the time of reaching out across the universe to join hands with the beings on other planets and on other planes.

Already, angels speak to us and aliens visit. This you can know to be true whether or not you have witnessed either. You may have never been to China, but you know it is there. People come and tell you they have seen it. They may have photographs and souvenirs. Regardless, you believe them. "Well," says the skeptic, "of course China exists. Any geography book will tell you that." Answer that the Bible says there are angels, and the skeptics scoff. The Bible is not as credible to them as a geography text. "Besides," the skeptic may say, "lots of people have been to China, they couldn't all have been making it up." Say that lots of people have seen angels, and the skeptic snorts, calls the people hysterics or the visions hallucinations.

In the Age of Aquarius, even the skeptics will believe—they, and all of us, will *know*.

The spirit of Aquarius requires that we unite with the universal spirit. To discover our oneness with everything in the vast cosmos links us to everything in the cosmos. Our travels may be in what we know as rocket ships or in variations of them, linking us to other beings on other planets; or they may be voyages of the mind, linking us with the great cosmic spirit and to all the spirits united with it. As we develop and expand our mental powers, increase our capacity for telepathy, and lift the veil of our unconscious abilities, we lose the need to move physically in search of knowledge. Merely entering the current of universal knowingness opens the door to all wisdom and knowledge of everything within the tapestry of time. That every known culture on Earth has accounts of angels is a testament to the reality of their existence. Once again, it defies the imagination, stretches the bounds of reason beyond the breaking limit, to suggest that every independent culture somehow imagined the existence of "winged messengers of God" who came to us in times of trouble and protected us in times of danger.

Could Mohammed have gotten his message from the angel Gabriel in the desert, *and* North American natives believe in winged "raven" and "eagle" people who carry messages from God, *and* Eskimos in the Arctic Circle believe that every child has a guardian spirit watching over it—all just by coincidence?

No, there has to be more to it than just chance. And there is. Angels are as real as you or me, but most of us are not ready to receive them in the way we would receive a neighbor from across the street who comes to call. Knowing that, angels hold back and watch from behind the veil of our limited view. Sudden, total illumination can be forever blinding to those who live in darkness. We see angels in times of real danger, in times of real distress, because at those times we open ourselves totally to God, the universe, and everything in it. When we are clinging to the edge of the cliff and feel our fingers slipping, that is when what little faith we may have had before turns into an absolute knowledge that there is a force that will lift us; we call out to God with every ounce of our being—and our call is heard. Somehow, something comes to our aid.

That is the Aquarian spirit in action: when faith turns to personal knowledge and we unite totally with the oneness of the universe; when we realize that we are all part of the totality and we connect with the universal spirit around us. In that instant, we glimpse the miracle that will be common in Aquarius; because once we connect totally with the universal spirit, there is no knowledge that is withheld. The angels appear.

Already, angels come to us. But they often come in the most unusual ways, so that it's hard to say whether we've met one, or been touched by one, or not. It's often easy to shrug off the touch of an angel as mere coincidence.

A friend of mine has been touched by angels. He's a reporter, with long experience in both print and television, a man given to probing, analytical questioning. He seeks proof rather than conjecture or whimsical fancy. Yet he has felt the work of angels.

The most recent time it happened was New Year's Eve, the closing night of 1995. He had to work and wasn't overly happy about the prospect of spending the night with a reporter's notebook in hand, asking questions of strangers, instead of in the company of his family. Still, responsibly, he went to work and was sent to cover the Orange Bowl Parade in downtown Miami. As do most of us on the night when one year ends and another begins, he found himself reflecting on his past accomplishments and his future direction. Even though he was working, he found himself pausing, nagged by self-doubts, questioning whether he had done anything meaningful with his life to this point, beyond bringing home a paycheck to provide for his wife and son.

He had done this before, of course; had even switched careers for a brief while a few years earlier, turning to teaching troubled, young, and potential dropouts. It had been rewarding, extremely demanding work that gave him much pleasure when he saw his students' successes and much pain when he saw their failures. Eventually, however, he felt the calling draw him back to reporting and at the close of a school year, he left teaching and returned to covering the news.

Still, this night, the doubts returned as he turned his analytical mind on himself. Then, suddenly, as the questions swirled inside his head, one of his former students appeared out of nowhere to stand beside him. The teenager smiled and introduced himself and went on to tell the man who had been his teacher the impact the experience had had on him. The boy had gone on with his studies instead of dropping out of school and was about to graduate from high school. Already, he said, he had been accepted for admittance to two very reputable universities and was considering his choice.

"You made the difference," the boy said. "You turned my life around. And we all really loved when you went into TV, so we could watch you all the time and know that you were right—there was more we all could be."

Then the boy thanked the man again, wished him a happy New Year, and disappeared into the crowd.

Was it a coincidence? Or was it an angel who heard my friend's doubts, heard his questions, and nudged the boy to go forward and say exactly what the man needed to hear?

The same man had another unusual experience a few months before the incident with the boy. He and his wife had bought a new home. It was more expensive than the one they lived in, the only one they had ever owned, and he was troubled. He tried not to let on, but even as they were moving, he wondered if they were doing the right thing. The die was cast, the old house was sold, they were packed and taking their things to the new one, and still he felt a tiny lick of fear in the pit of his stomach. Would they be able to afford the new place? Weren't they just fine where they had been?

He loaded the last of their belongings in his car, slammed the door shut, and turned to look one last time at the house they were leaving, still wondering if what was happening was truly best for them.

And as he looked back at the house, suddenly, out of nowhere, a peacock stepped to the peak of the house's roof. A *peacock!* This is in the middle of Miami, in the city, not in some rural farmland where all manner of animals roam. My friend turned to his nephew and asked, "Do you see that?"

"Yes," the startled nephew said.

"What do you see?" my friend asked, becoming the reporter again, still unsure and not wanting to taint the answer with the form of the question.

"A peacock," his nephew sputtered. "On the roof."

What could this mean? My friend didn't know, but he knew it was good. And in that moment, the burden of his questions lifted and he knew that he was supposed to move to the new house.

I call both incidents the work of angels and show them as examples of how angels come into our lives, touch us, and leave again without us being sure that they were angels at all.

Has some stranger performed a truly kind act for you, then disappeared before you even got the chance to thank him or her? Has there been a moment when you thought desperately that you needed help and, suddenly, you got it? Have you been driving or walking, lost in a bad part of some strange city, wondering how you were going to get out of there without getting into trouble, getting robbed, or worse and in that exact instant that you thought all hope was lost has someone who didn't really seem to belong there stepped forward and offered directions—before you even asked?

Was it, really, just a coincidence? Really?

Sometimes, angels come unmistakably. They come bathed in an intensely glowing light, with wings or not, and as they approach you feel a sense of such sheer, overpowering peace and serenity that you know everything is going to be all right.

There was the case of the Florida boy who went off alone to go fishing near his home one day and was bitten by a rattlesnake. As the massive dose of venom rushed through his bloodstream, the boy felt himself losing consciousness and falling, knowing he was too far from any home to reach help, so far that any call for help would be lost in the wind without anyone hearing, and that he could not possibly make it back to his own home. But as he lay on the ground, he suddenly felt large hands lifting him and he was floating, rushing at incredible speed through the swamp, carried by someone or something whose feet didn't even seem to touch the ground. Everything seemed dreamy, but he was aware of being surrounded by a bright glow as he was whisked to his own front porch and deposited at the door where he could call for help.

His family rushed him to the hospital and the boy was saved. Later, he told them what had happened, about the stranger who carried him to the door to be saved. But no one else had seen the glowing stranger. Whoever or whatever it was simply vanished into thin air when the door opened and the boy cried out for help.

Sometimes angels come as rescuers; sometimes they come as messengers. That can happen in our dreams or when we are wide awake. But you must open yourself to them. If they come to you there is a reason. Even if they don't, you need to examine your life and ask if you are doing all that you can, ask whether you are fulfilling your purpose on this plane. This is of the utmost importance as we move into the next millennium. We each are here at this specific moment for a special reason, at the very least to help all of us move swiftly beyond the time of crisis and into the new era. Once there, we will all be called upon to advance the ideals of peace and humanity. Once there, as we make union with the universal spirit, we will make union with the angels and aliens, and with our lost ancestors who long ago preceded us and joined with the great cosmic consciousness—or, if the legends are true, went into space.

The first account of the lost continent of Atlantis comes to us from Plato. In *Timaeus*, he wrote that long before even what we now call Ancient Greece existed, "there lay an island which was larger than Libya and Asia together ... Now in this island of Atlantis there existed a confederation of kings, of great and marvelous power ..."

At one time, Plato wrote, the forces of Atlantis tried to use their might against the ancestors of the Greeks—ancestors so ancient that none of the Greeks of Plato's time even knew of their existence—but they were repelled. The story is told by a man from another land, according to Plato, and the reason the knowledge has been lost is because "there have been and there will be many and diverse destructions of mankind ..." caused by the "shifting of bodies in the heavens which move round the earth, and a destruction of the things on the earth by fierce fire, which recurs at long intervals."

At one such time, Plato wrote, "there occurred portentous earthquakes and floods, and one grievous day and night befell them, when the whole body of your warriors was swallowed up by the earth, and the island of Atlantis in like manner was swallowed up by the sea and vanished ..."

If Plato's was the only account we had of Atlantis, it might be dismissed as fantasy, as a literary device created for the sole purpose of making a point. But ancient legends around the world suggest that Atlantis did in fact exist at some time in the distant past, a huge continent stretching across most of what we now call the Atlantic Ocean, one end near the Iberian Peninsula and northern Africa and the other near the southern reaches of North America, Central America, and the northern end of South America. The Toltecs and Nahautlacas, ancient and now lost tribes that preceded the Aztecs and Mayas in Central America and southern Mexico, both described their birthplaces as being a lost land to the East. The Toltecs said they originally came from a land called Aztlan or Atlan. The Nahautlacas said their birthplace was Aztlan. The Aztecs too told of their ancestors having lived in a place known as Aztlan. The Paria of Venezuela said that their homeland, a large island in the ocean, was destroyed by a catastrophe. The name they gave to their village in Venezuela was a tribute to that lost homeland: Atlan.

In North America, the Mandan tribe held religious ceremonies every year that began with a solitary man, painted all white, approaching the village. The man was called Nu-mohk-muck-a-nah, which means the first or only man. During the ceremony, the person playing the role of Nu-mohk-muck-a-nah went to each lodge and recounted to the lodge's owner the story of how he had escaped a universal catastrophe, a terrible flood that covered the Earth, and landed in his "big canoe on a high mountain in the west."

The story comes to us by way of Ignatius Donnelly, based on the eyewitness account of George Catlin, who met the tribe in the mid-nineteenth century. But the similarities between the big canoe and Noah's Ark are unmistakable. The fact that the Mandan legend has its only survivor of the Great Flood head west from his homeland also is supported by other Native American myths, which place the original land in what would now be the Atlantic Ocean.

The *Oera Linda Book*, which contains the traditional history of the Frisian peoples of northern Europe, also contains an account of a once-great land that disappeared into the ocean after a massive earthquake: "Aldland, called by the seafaring people Atland, disappeared, and the wild waves rose so high over hill and dale that everything was buried in the sea."

The Celts said their ancestors came from a land known as Avalon, which was finally added to the kingdom of the sea god. The Basques contend that their ancestors came from a land known as Atlaintika. The Portuguese believe that Atlantida once existed in the ocean west of Portugal and that the Azores are all that are left of that land's mountain peaks. The Spanish call the same land Atalaya and say that the Canary Islands are what remain of it.

The North African Berbers maintain the legend of a once-rich land called Attala, which sank beneath the sea but that they expect someday to rise again. The Phoenicians spoke of an island of vast wealth called Antilla. And the ancient sacred texts of India describe a continent called Attala.

Edgar Cayce, the clairvoyant healer of Virginia Beach, also spoke of Atlantis, describing its culture as one of the most advanced civilizations on Earth. Its people, he said, metamorphosed directly from the spirit plane into human form and drifted increasingly from their spiritual ideals as they became more and more attached to power and the material world. They suffered a total of three devastations, according to Cayce, one around 50,000 B.C.; then again about 28,500 B.C., when the continent broke into three islands; and finally, about 10,500 B.C., when all three islands sank into the ocean and disappeared. The last appears to be the one mentioned by Plato.

Modern Atlantologists, as they are known, believe that a few Atlantean survivors escaped the final destruction and moved on to other lands, among them Egypt and the Mexican Yucatán, where they helped develop cultures. In both places, we see pyramids and advanced astrological and mathematical arts developing, apparently independently, some two thousand years before the birth of Christ. The earliest stepped pyramid, a precursor to the classic pyramid most of us think of when we think of Egypt, was built as a tomb about 2725 B.C. Recent excavations of early Mayan structures, built between 1500 and 1600 B.C., suggest that they were originally used as tombs, too.

That this could be so also is suggested by the first-century historian Diodorus Siculus, as cited by Robert Scrutton in his book *The Other Atlantis*, who wrote: "The Egyptians were strangers, who, in remote times, settled on the banks of the Nile, bringing with them the civilization of their mother country, the art of writing, and a polished language. They had come from the direction of the setting sun and were the most ancient of men."

The migration of the Atlanteans to other shores, either before or after the final cataclysm that sent the lost continent to the ocean floor, also helps explain the similarity of certain basic words in a multitude of diverse and geographically distant cultures around the world. Charles Berlitz noted in *Atlantis* the resemblance of the word for "father" in several languages as an example. The Quechua Indians say *taita* for *father;* the Basques, *aita;* the Dakotah, *atey;* in Tagalog, it is *tatay.* And in Samoan, Central Mexican Indian dialects, colloquial Latin, Romanian, Slovak, Maltese, and Sinhalese, it's *tata.*

According to the accounts of Cayce and others, the Atlanteans harnessed amazing technological power, learning to capture incredible solar energy in rubylike crystals (which sounds a lot like the workings of a ruby laser, which wasn't even invented until more than fifteen years after Cayce's death) and capable of using the Earth's geomagnetic forces to their own ends. In the end, however, the Atlanteans used their power to battle one another and somehow unleashed their technological power in a devastating manner, setting off the final cataclysm that sent them sinking deep to the ocean's bottom. The rising waters caused by the suddenly sinking continent could be, conceivably, the cause of the great floods mentioned in both Sumerian and Biblical writings.

In his book *Atlantis—from Legend to Discovery,* Robert Hale cites Ovid, the Roman poet, who lends support to this theory and to the possibility that at least some of the first Atlanteans left this planet and headed into space, writing that: "There was such wickedness once on earth that Justice *fled to the sky* ... Neptune smote the earth with his trident and the earth shivered and shook ... Soon there was no telling land from sea. Under the water the sea nymphs Nereides were staring in amazement at woods, houses and cities. Nearly all men perished by water, and those who escaped the water, having no food, died of hunger" [emphasis added].

The leap into space would also explain the precise astronomical knowledge held by the Dogon tribe of Mali. Their peoples helped to form the powerful and culturally advanced Mali empire that reigned from about 1200 to nearly 1500, which we remember for its university at Timbuktu in West Africa, one of the most advanced cultural and learning centers of the world. But to this day, the Dogons preserve their ancient religious rituals and the beliefs passed on from prehistory, those born in the cloudy era before their written language marked time; among them, concepts of the universe that we are only now discovering to be stunningly accurate. How they knew remains beyond our ability to explain, but for time immemorial, long before our space probes ventured beyond our atmosphere, before even the invention of the telescope, members of this tribe maintained that the Moon was a dead sphere in space, that rings circled Saturn, that Jupiter had four moons, and that the planets revolved around the Sun. The Dogon legends say that visitors from space delivered this knowledge to them, by way of Egypt.

In any case, I agree with the visionaries who say that many of us here now are actually incarnations of Atlantean souls, returned to help guide us as we face many of the same challenges they did just before their continent disappeared and lead us into "a new millennium of peace and hope."

Nonetheless, some believe that one day we will discover the records of this great lost civilization in Egypt, left there by survivors of the final Atlantean destruction. Others believe that the survivors not only made their way to other lands, but to other planets as well.

I believe that both are true. But as the truth of legends are gilded through time, we will discover that the Atlanteans had pushed out into the heavens before the final battle, colonizing worlds distant from ours, planting the seed of humanity in remote realms of the universe. When the final cataclysm came, those colonies were cut off, to continue an independent history; and when the final cataclysm came and Atlantis was lost, a few survivors made their way to surrounding lands, carrying with them what they could of their culture and their knowledge to merge with that of the cultures that took them in.

And I know that now, on the verge of that New Millennium of peace and hope, as we progress into this age of enlightenment, when lost knowledge and new knowledge both are opened to us, we are also on the brink of discovering the true history of Atlantis.

It may come because the era ahead will be the great age of space exploration, and as we push into the stars, we will link up with our past. The Atlanteans, their lesson learned, may be waiting for this crucial moment in our development to reunite with us. Rather than inundating us with the sum of their knowledge at a time when we were less than prepared to receive it, at a time when we were still lacking in the proper spiritual development, they may have patiently preserved their wisdom in some distant place, awaiting our arrival. The wise know that everyone learns when they are ready to learn, not because someone else is ready to teach. No one is led to knowledge; everybody seeks it for themselves and finds it only when they are ready to receive it.

Knowing that, it makes sense that the Atlanteans would reserve their technological knowledge until we are spiritually ready to handle it or until we reached the point in our advancement that we had developed similar tools powerful enough to take us to them and faced the challenge of learning to use them responsibly.

If that is so, then some of the "aliens" we encounter may not be aliens at all, but our ancestors. But even if that is so, it is also true that some of us who walk today have walked before on the now-lost continent of Atlantis. We all have been here before. In the great cycle of reincarnations, we come to this plane to continue with our lessons; when our bodies die, we reunite with the celestial spirit to await a new incarnation. It is highly probable that at least some of us were here before during the time of Atlantis and are now returning to once again face the challenge—to learn the lesson—of finding the peaceful combination of science and spirituality. Some of them—some of you—will lead the rest of us in the new awakening, bringing the wisdom of the past so that we may avoid the painful lesson of Atlantis; and some will help lead us to the lost Atlantean record.

We may discover the truth about Atlantis in Egypt *and* in space. Either way, as we move into the New Millennium and lift the veils within our minds, we are on the brink of recovering the lost record within ourselves.

Within the great collective unconscious—what has been called the *Akashic* records or the "Book of Life"—lies every instant of history. Every event, every movement, every sound, every thought has been collected indelibly in that great tapestry of time. As we connect with that universal oneness of spiritual being, we will share in every spark of its total knowingness. Not only will we each know and remember our own past lives and lessons, we will all share the totality of the past. Like a drop of water falling into the ocean, we will become one with it all, completely incorporated in the whole and with all contained therein. We will know all that is and all that ever was, including Atlantis, in a single burst of *knowing*.

# 9

---

# Birth Signs and the New Millennium: Discovering Your Individual Mission

The spirit of the age touches all of us equally. We each are saturated with the essence of Aquarius as we step into the New Millennium. But each person still responds to their own birth sign. Every one of us feels the energy of Aquarius, and it drives each of us to maximize our contribution—to draw upon our inborn talents—within the character of our birth sign.

## ARIES

---

Arians are the torchbearers of the new era. They are pioneering and adventurous by nature, clearcut and forceful, enterprising, direct, and courageous. As we step further into the New Age with a new way of thinking and living and cooperating together, it is in the character of the Arians to step to the forefront and take us beyond what is and into what will be. In our communities, they will be the captains of change, pulling us with them into the new way of the Age of Aquarius; in our world, they will be the explorers, digging deep into the unknown reaches of the Earth and its jungles, deep into its tundras and its seas, to bring out the hidden fruits of our planet for all to share; and, in this new age of exploration, where we push beyond our world and into the vastness of the universe, they will be in the vanguard of our voyages, our guides, our guardians, and our planetary pioneers.

Arians also do well as psychologists and psychiatrists, and as our voyages of discovery take us also deep into ourselves, they will be the explorers and pioneers there as well, boldly pushing beyond what is known to help us discover the hidden well of power that lies within us all and to lead us back to our connection with the forces that surround us. Whatever is hidden, the Arians will seek to uncover; whatever our limits, they will seek to expand. Whether it is discovering what lies beyond the edge of the known in the universe, delivering a cure hidden in a flower deep in the rain forest, or finding a new way of living in harmony with our environment, the Arians will be our leaders and our guides.

Their inborn need for freedom, their resistance to restriction, also make the Arians perfect for the task of teaching us new forms of government, where individual and collective freedoms are paramount; to end the laws that bind us and bring about the laws that free us; and to show us all that true freedom begins within us, once we are free of our self-imposed restraints. The Arians will open whole new worlds, without and within, and whole new ways of thinking.

## TAURUS

Those born in the sign of Taurus are those who bring to fruition what someone else has invented. Taurus is Earth, and its character is patient. The mission of Taurus is to patiently work and mold and bring into being that which another less patient sign has created. Taurus is more tranquil, more serene, more calm, and therefore more capable of taking the time necessary to give substance to ideas. Some other sign draws the blueprint, some other is the architect with the pen, but Taurus is the master mason who turns the design into a finished structure, brick by brick. Taurus has both the manual potential and the innate talent to construct the castles that others conceived. Without that Taurean trait, the dreams would remain unrealized, the plans would remain on paper.

The Age of Aquarius is an age of tremendous creativity in all regards. We will unite to build whole new societies and systems, whole new ways. But what others envision in the New Age, Taureans will make real. A person born under the sign of Taurus may show its influence in the most literal manner, setting the bricks that make the new, ecologically conscious housing of the future; or they may show their talent for construction in a more figurative way, taking their place as leaders in the New Millennium, filling the halls of government and making sure that the outlines for a new society drawn up on reams of bureaucratic paper become real and permanent procedures for progress.

Taureans are practical and reliable, able in business, and capable of great endurance, like the bull that gave the sign its name. Being of the Earth, Taureans are likely to return to it in the New Millennium, turning their natural abilities to horticulture or agriculture. This predisposes them to an important role in the New Age, that of revitalizing the Earth, of repairing the damage done by the destructive ways of the past. Taurus is ruled by Venus, and the feminine, loving character of Venus will be positively charged by the energy of Aquarius, promoting a profound sense of nurturing in our relationship with Mother Earth. As the New Age demands that we renew our connection with the environment, as it instills an ever higher regard for nature, Taureans will be crucial players in turning those ideals into ways of life.

Naturally, Taureans also have an affinity for all of the building trades, and as we look for new, less destructive ways to live, it will be Taureans who will build the structures that work in conjunction with the land and nature, that utilize nonpolluting forms of energy such as wind or the Sun. Constructing, manufacturing, beautifying the world around them—all these things are extremely well aspected for Taureans under the increasing influence of Aquarius.

Taureans also are adept at business, inclining them toward careers as financiers or bankers. Those vocations too are of supreme importance in the New Age. Aquarius inspires us to develop new economic models that consider more acutely the concepts of humanity and unity. As the Piscean concept of conquest, of taking, dies under the pressure of the coming era, new systems take their place. These new ways of business can already be seen taking shape in the theories of global economy. Countries today realize that they are all interconnected, that the economic ills and imbalances of one affect all, that the prosperity of one is shared by others. Eventually, we will realize that when we all prosper, we *all* prosper. Keeping any one or any group down is a disservice to all. Denying any one or any group the opportunity to contribute diminishes the success of the whole. This will not bring a rebirth of the failed concept of communism—all *isms* are taboo in the New Age—but a totally new concept in keeping with the creative and independent and freedom-loving nature of Aquarius. It is enlightened business that comes into being, not a return to chained labor. As these concepts evolve in the new era, Taureans will be the most likely to participate in giving them form and making them concrete.

## G E M I N I

The children of Gemini articulate the Taurean constructions. Geminis are the great communicators, along with Sagittarians, and in the New Age they are the ones who will be seen shouting from the rooftops. They will write the words and speak the speeches, extolling the praises of the New Millennium, exhorting us to join with them on the path to the New Age.

Geminis are among those who benefit the most in the Age of Aquarius because they too are of the air. They not only flow into but also with the spirit of the times; and their minds will burst—explode—with thousands of new ideas that, in typically Gemini fashion, they will proclaim loudly to everyone.

Communications are extremely important in the coming era. Through communication comes understanding. By linking us together to share ideas, good communications help us diminish our differences and expand our sense of unity and fraternity. Geminis, then, share the mission of not only communicating their own ideas, but helping us build our means of communications, bringing us closer to that global village.

People born under the sign of Gemini naturally gravitate toward the communications fields, and now it will be even more so. But where before they may have been telephone operators, now they build telephone systems and satellite links. They wire our computers together so that someone in Calcutta, India, can exchange ideas as easily with someone in Ketchum, Idaho, as they can with their next-door neighbor. Geminis will help build the Internet into a gateway to knowledge for everyone, everywhere.

Aquarius benefits the positive traits of Gemini, so those born under its sign will be even more compelled to pursue their natural talent as teachers, communicating the message of the New Millennium in our colleges and helping the young to find their own talents. As our antiquated systems of education crumble in the New Age, Geminis will be among the ones helping to bring about the teaching methods of the future, when educators will not seek to impose their will on their students, but instead will help them recognize their own abilities and guide them toward the vocations that they themselves select.

Their affinity for language and overpowering need to communicate drives Geminis naturally into careers as journalists, broadcasters, and commentators. The New Age requires many speakers to carry the message, people who will influence without forcing, and Geminis are supremely suited for the job. Their skill at expression will allow them to show others the way, so that each may find it on their own. This is of the utmost importance in the New Age: everyone must be allowed to find the way for themselves; others, such as the Geminis, can illuminate the path, but no one can lead anyone else to knowledge—they must find it for themselves. This will be a challenge the Geminis will love, and one they will take on with zeal. Geminis love change, and in Aquarius they have the chance to use their communicative skills to bring about the change. It certainly helps that Geminis also love being guides, which is why so many of them tend to be chauffeurs or navigators—helping others find their way to where they are going, but never deciding for the other where that should be.

## CANCER

Cancerians need to be protective and maternal. They are tenacious, kind, sympathetic, and sensitive. Everything that is built by Taurus and proclaimed by Geminis is warmed in the heart of Cancer. Cancerians tend to be withdrawn and closed, but in the Age of Aquarius, they peel away that sensitivity and burst forth with strength. Before, everything wounded them. In the New Millennium, they become emotionally fortified. With that newfound inner strength, Cancerians become the caretakers of the Aquarian spirit, nurturing the rest of us as we go through the times of trouble that lead into the New Millennium.

The innate inclination of Cancerians is to become nurses, curators, and caretakers. As such, using their excellent memories and love of history, they are the perfect guardians to guide us by reminding us of what has failed, so that we will find our way to new systems. And when we stumble, the Cancerians will be the ones there to care for us so that we may resume our voyage. Their compassion for others is magnified by the energy of the New Age, and in their quiet resolve many of us will find examples for ourselves.

In the Age of Pisces, Cancerians also were drawn to careers at sea or involving the sea. In some cases this is likely to continue, perhaps even be magnified, and in those cases Cancerians are likely to be the ones who help us find new resources for feeding ourselves in keeping with the ecologically inclined emphasis of Aquarius; some may even become involved in adapting the power of the sea to power our cities in environmentally sound ways. But it is very likely that many Cancerians will feel their love of the flowing seas and the natural pull of the Moon that rules them, leading them to voyage in the new frontier across oceans of space. In this manner, Aquarius, the Water Bearer, will

open new ways and places for the Cancerians to express their
tenacious characters and powerful imaginations.


## L E O

Powerful and mighty, Leos benefit by being born under the
sign of Aquarius' natural polarity. Both Leo and Aquarius
lend their nature to the New Millennium. Where Aquarius is
independent, Leo is a good organizer; where Aquarius is
humanitarian, Leo is magnanimous; where Aquarius is reform-
ing and progressive, Leo is broad-minded and expansive. They
are perfect complements. Leo's enthusiasm, creativity, and
power are the perfect catalysts to push forward Aquarius'
inventions.

But Leo's real brilliance in the New Age comes in the area
of love, of unions. With the loyalty inherent to the sign—
anyone born under its influence will gladly be a willing slave
to a master he or she respects—Leo will emphasize the spirit
of unity in the New Millennium. Aquarius, of course, loves
independence and freedom, so there will be no slaves in the
New Age. But the cooperation of Leo and Aquarius will
color the entire era, serving as shining examples for the rest
of us.

Leos are the stars of the big top. They love acting, dancing,
and publicity. They love to roar and to have everyone hear them.
Their devotion to the objects of their affections and respect
makes them the perfect promoters of Aquarian reforms and
ideals. Leos are the optimistic, cheerful people who bring sun-
shine into other people's lives; and in the Age of Aquarius, that
brilliant light takes on a whole new meaning as Leos steadfastly

work to bring illumination to all. Leos tend to be extremely
capable organizers of other people, another trait that will lead
them into new dramatic parts as role models for the rest of us
as we move into the New Millennium. Naturally hard workers
with the lion's strength and dedication, they also serve as models for those around them.

Leos, like the lion that gives the sign its name, tend to dote
lovingly but firmly over the young. That makes them naturals as
teachers and youth leaders. In the New Age, this will not
change. Leos will be in the vanguard of change in education,
guiding children, especially older children, in the new philosophy of the era. As with any of the signs, it is the positive traits
of Leo that are emphasized in the New Age under the influence
of Aquarius.

## VIRGO

Those born under the sign of Virgo bring their discriminat-
ing, analytical, and meticulous manner to the forefront in the
New Millennium. Virgos lean toward the sciences and just
about any career connected with health and hygiene. What
could be more favorable in the coming age of dedication to
our planet, at the time when science and spirituality join
hands?

Virgo is an Earth sign, associated with the virginal, the pure.
As we reclaim the lost beauty of Mother Earth and try to
return our home planet to a more pristine state, Virgoan scientists will take premiere positions in making this goal a reality.
Virgoans are natural gardeners, in the literal and symbolic
sense. They are the ones who will bring back the flowering gar-

dens of bygone ages; they are the ones best suited to make the deserts bloom.

Virgos are natural gardeners—literally, tending both fields and flower beds, and, symbolically, nurturing the growth of love and hope.

As we look for new forms of medicinal and natural cures, Virgo again leads the way in the New Millennium. The combinations of their predilections—on the one hand, their love of the virginal and pure, especially in the Earth; and, on the other hand, their disposition for careers in health and hygiene—come together with explosive dynamism within the energizing impact of Aquarius, to find and deliver new means of healing and guarding our health. Aquarius is the age of returning to the ways of nature, of realizing that the Earth provides a cure for every ill. In the Age of Aquarius, Virgos assume their natural role and help us discover nature's hidden treasures.

According to the myth that lends its name to the sign, Virgo was the goddess of justice, an eminently requisite quality in the New Millennium. As Aquarius compels us toward tolerance, Virgo drives us toward equity—and together they impel us toward humanity and fraternity. As we restructure our systems of justice and laws, Virgos will help recall the myth and help bring the golden age back to Earth again. Their analytical minds and sense of justice will make them perfect for examining our existing laws and regulations, to decide what is useful and what should be discarded. The New Age is born on the ashes of the old, it is true—what has been must be destroyed to make way for the new—but the Aquarian Age is a positive age, and this will be positive destruction. It takes the help of Virgo to bring the Phoenix back from the ashes, to decide what is just and should remain, and to decide what is detrimental and should be thrown out.

## LIBRA

---

Librans, as the children of an air sign, are particularly well aspected in the New Millennium, since it is the Age of Aquarius, another air sign. The essence of Libra, balance, is embodied in the constellation which bears its name, the scales. Librans balance the scales of justice, find equity for opponents, and seek the level and familiar setting of order. Obviously, their love of balance and justice compels Librans to seek harmony and peace. To do this, Librans strive for diplomacy in all of their dealings, although their compulsion to express themselves in all facets of life sometimes makes this difficult. Still, reinforced by the positive energy of the New Age, Librans are likely to serve as the peacemakers, with a central role in the shaping and evolution of the golden age ahead. As an air sign, Libra dominates the mental processes, and the powerful effect of Aquarius upon them will make Librans burst with creative ideas. They work best in partnership with others, and their sense of justice makes them ideally suited to aid in the task of restructuring our system of courts and laws, a critical function in bringing about the environment in which the Aquarian society will truly thrive.

Librans also are extremely intuitive, a result of air and mental influences. This gives them tremendous gifts as psychics, whose powers will be expanded greatly under the magnifying force of the planets in the new era. This will perhaps become the Librans' primary role in the New Age—as the visionaries who see beyond our physical plane and into the spiritual world. As those who see the way clearly, combined with their innate need to express themselves tactfully, they will work as the grand partners in illuminating the path into the New Millennium. As diplomats, they will serve in their other great capacity, eliminating the divisiveness of the past to bring all countries together in unity.

## S C O R P I O

Scorpio is the symbol of life and death, and of sex. But although others often regard Scorpios warily, all of their attributes are in fact expressions of their powerful passion for life itself. Scorpios are passionate in everything they do, and forever express themselves forcefully with overpowering endurance.

Their drive and relentless pursuit of their goals make Scorpios formidable in whatever field they aspire to, as long as they find it personally challenging. Scorpios make excellent surgeons and psychologists and also do well in areas requiring intense research, such as academics. In the New Age, many Scorpios may find the adventure and intensity of space exploration magnetically attractive and a perfect place to invest their prodigious talents. As surgeons, they will wield their scalpels in new ways, knowing that the patient knows his or her own cure and that the knife cuts best when it cuts least, teaching others that knowing when not to cut is as important as knowing when to. As psychologists, they will draw upon their formidable intuitive powers to delve into the psyches of their patients and lead the troubled out from the fog of their minds. They will be professors with passion, driving their students to go beyond what is known; researchers of renown, peeling away the veils of mystery, relentlessly digging through the layers of the unknown, taking us with them into new realms of knowledge.

But no matter what career they choose, Scorpios hold a special talent, one of overriding importance in the coming age. All

Scorpios are possessed of tremendous psychic powers and are profoundly spiritual. If this was true in the past, it is even more so now because Scorpio is ruled by Pluto, which is getting even more expanded powers from its position in Sagittarius, where it will continue to reside as we cross into the New Millennium. As we go deeper into the era of Aquarius and feel the cosmic current flowing over and through every one of us, their sensitivity to the emanations will make these passionate Scorpios invaluable guides for the rest of us. Their inner antennas will tingle and tune in far ahead of those of others, making them the perfect spiritual counselors to help the rest of us balance and tune our own antenna to the revelations in the cosmic tapestry. Theirs will be the antennas that vibrate with the energy of the universal spirit, and they will serve as the messengers of the people.

## SAGITTARIUS

Sagittarians are the proclaimers of truth in the New Age. They are the travelers, the optimistic and philosophical freedom lovers of the zodiac, and the torchbearers of the future occupying the ninth house, the house of the master, the right hand of God. Sagittarians often spend their entire lives traveling physically and spiritually, always in search of themselves. Sagittarius is the sign of the future, the promise of humanity, and the wandering nature of those born under it finds direction in the time at hand, taking firm steps toward the common objective awaiting us.

With Pluto in their sign exploding with the energy of the unconscious and the spiritual, Sagittarians will lead the journey inward, into ourselves, and outward to the stars. The celestial centaur represented by their constellation is the powerful mix of strong physical energy and deep intellectual pursuit. The myth behind the naming of the constellation is that Sagittarius is the centaur Cheiron, who raised Jason, Achilles, and Aeneas and was famous as a prophet, a doctor, and a scholar.

In all of these fields again will Sagittarians play important roles in the New Age, both literally and figuratively. They will be prophets and doctors and scholars, of course, but they will also be prophetic guides, healers, and teachers of humanity in the spiritual sense as well. Their visionary powers are especially enhanced as we cross into the New Millennium, and their philosophical nature and voyager's hearts will enhance their desire to probe the deepest regions of their inner beings. They will emerge from their journeys, bursting with the desire to share their newfound wisdom with the world, and lead us all toward the union with the universal spirit that lies within and around us.

Sagittarians love exploring in every way, and their love of travel and adventure is also apt to lead them to join the growing field of space exploration, the rest of us trailing in their wake. Sagittarians lean toward careers as teachers, professors, philosophers, priests, lawyers, and writers—anywhere they can share and use their knowledge. And here too Sagittarians will be potent contributors in the New Millennium. They will reach out to explore, to discover, and to gather knowledge, then bring back their findings to help shape the future.

## CAPRICORN

Capricorns are the ones who will lay the economic foundation in the new era. They are reliable, determined, ambitious, patient, and persevering. Like the mountain goats that are the symbol of this sign, Capricorns always rise to the summit steadily, patiently, picking their way from crag to crag to reach the pinnacle in whatever endeavor they've chosen. They are the true servants of humanity, bringing steady calm in times of emergency, trouble, or war, knowing in their interiors that no matter how precarious things may seem, there is a way to continue climbing toward our goal if we apply ourselves persistently.

The vocations that appeal to Capricorns are generally those that demand diligent dedication, such as civil service, mathematics, politics, engineering, science, building, and administration. As we strive to restructure all of our systems in the New Millennium, Capricorns will characteristically apply their tenacious characters to building solid foundations for the future, always bearing in mind their goal of serving the totality of humanity.

In politics and administration, they will be the ones called upon to ensure that the needs of all are addressed in government; the ones who bring about a true democracy where all people contribute and are served. In business, they will take us determinedly toward the ideal of progress, proving that everyone climbing to the summit helps us all to reach the top. As builders, their practicality will be enhanced by the inventiveness of Aquarius so that we may find the best application of the materials at hand, building solid bases for all of our endeavors without undermining our progress by damaging the planet that supports us.

Capricorns have an inborn skill for handling large, complicated enterprises, which is perfect for the global task at hand. What could be more enriching and challenging than helping to rebuild everything, to make a whole new world based on the precepts of compassion and fraternity? In this, their ability as architects will also be much in demand, not only as designers of buildings, but as architects of the New Age, helping to plan and raise the structure that will guide us into the golden age of humanity.

## A Q U A R I U S

Aquarians, of course, are especially blessed in the New Millennium. This is their age, their time, and they will shine brilliantly throughout, setting the standards that all others aspire to. Aquarius is the sign of excellence, of humanity, represented by a human figure, the Water Bearer, pouring out knowledge on the Earth to saturate all of us. They are the bearers of the universal conscience, the cosmic consciousness, and the sacred eternal knowledge. Flowing from those born under this sign are the waters of wisdom and, as an air sign, they also reign over electricity and electronics.

In this practical manner, Aquarians will excel as the inventors and creators of tools that will take us into the most distant realms of space, of tools that will ease our labor, give us more freedom, and link us in universal unity.

Aquarians also are highly spiritual—even more so now—and they will be the true leaders of the coming era, showing us that the path to peace and evolution comes through a knowledge of ourselves, so that we may connect to the wisdom of the cosmos.

They are the creators, the inventors, the reformers, the intellectual humanitarians. Intelligent and intuitive, Aquarians will show their originality in a brilliant burst of ideas that breaks totally with the way things have been done; they will show us *how* things can be done. Aquarians will find their way into every field where they can bring their vision of the future closer to reality.

In politics, they will be the speakers in defense of the oppressed, the visionaries demanding reform, and the social architects raising the standard of living for all. In education, they will illuminate the realms of knowledge for all, so that each may select the path to their own personal enlightenment. In the arts, they will paint the images of paradise—with brushes, with words, and with music—that will guide us as we convert these images into realities.

Aquarians love to feel free and to soar, making them natural pilots. Prodded by the energy of their age, the Aquarian love of space that today makes them astronomers will tomorrow make them the pilots of intergalactic craft, carrying humanity into the infinite reaches of the universe.

Their intrinsically spiritual bent will also be exalted in the Age of Aquarius, and those ruled by that sign will bring the ultimate understanding of the universal essence to all humanity. They are the seekers of all-encompassing knowledge—of *knowing*—that goes beyond faith and belief; the seekers of truth. In this their age, Aquarians will discover that which all humanity has sought for all time and deliver that knowledge for all people.

## P I S C E S

Pisces is the last sign of the zodiac and the sign of the dying age. But rather than being maligned or oppressed by the death of their age and the birth of the new, the positive Piscean traits are elevated by the energy of Aquarius. Now comes the time for Pisceans to liberate themselves, to break free of their chains. They will feel the dissolution of all the negative that they've been in the past and feel themselves transformed into the examples of the new era. Piscean compassion, humility, sympathy, sensitivity, and intuition come to the fore, to lead us to the Christian ideals of living in peace with one another and joining with the universal spirit. Pisceans help us find our inner divinity, that connection to the cosmos and to our virtues that ties us inseparably to everything and everyone around us.

It is the Pisceans who bring us to the discovery that we are all the children of God, especially after their ruling planet, Neptune, joins Uranus in the sign of Aquarius in 1998. The birth of Christ signaled the commencement of the Age of Pisces and exemplified the positive characteristics of the sign. Naturally, Pisceans tend toward careers as priests, as spiritual guides, and that will be stressed even more in the coming age. But now Pisceans will not become martyrs, but the true masters of spiritual truth, able to deliver their message to the world and lead us to our spiritual rebirth.

Their compassion for others often draws Pisceans into fields as caregivers, nurses, doctors. Now, combined with their strong spiritual nature, Pisceans will implement their knowledge that within us lies a healing force for all of our diseases, changing us from patients waiting to be cured to partners who work with professionals to cure ourselves.

Characteristically, Pisceans will retain their love of the sea. They are the fishes of the zodiac, born under a water sign, doubly compelled to plumb the depths and to bring us the discovery of what is hidden beneath. Many will continue their service to people in this way, uncovering the wealth of resources below the waves that will benefit all humanity without harming nature.

But their talent for diving far below the surface also shows itself in their deeply spiritual nature, in their need to reach down to the profundities of their inner beings to discover the treasures therein. All Pisceans are bathed in an inner light, the light of illumination that wells up from within and draws them to the spiritual. Deep inside every Piscean is the quiet knowledge of who we are, why we are here, and what we are supposed to do. They hold a uniquely peculiar understanding of the true cosmic laws, and as the writers and poets of humanity, they have the special mission of sharing their knowledge with the rest of us.

As an age of the Earth, Aquarius extends its effect over all of us, no matter what our birth sign may be. It brings out the most positive of our inborn traits and impels us to put them to the service of all humanity. In the New Millennium, we each bear a special responsibility to ourselves and to our neighbors. We each must discover our unique and individual purpose to make it our mission in life. This will take longer for some than for others, but it is a necessity for all, a requisite for the New Age. Those who resist, who deny the Age of Aquarius, shall pass away with the old age without recognizing the glory of the new, because it is impossible to resist the power of the universe or to ignore our place in it.

Those who persist, who drive themselves to maximize their unique talents in the coming millennium, will occupy special—and sacred—positions in the New Age.

# 10

## Children of the New Age

The children of the New Age, those born and those to be born, are the privileged ones. They come to this world already touched and blessed by the spirit of the New Millennium, closer to the universal spirit and closer to their discovery of it.

For them, the door to the unconscious is already open. The drive to dive deep into their inner selves compels them to seek to know for themselves. They no longer want to accept beliefs; they want to build their own beliefs.

As their parents, we can learn from them, open ourselves to their lessons instead of forcing our lessons on them; or we can complicate their journey to discovery by imposing our beliefs on them, limiting their vision with our perception of what is possible and impossible, and closing the doors of their minds with the locks of our limited comprehension.

Scientists are delving deeper than ever before into the workings of that elusive thing called our minds. Their discoveries prove that the complicated mass of neural interconnections within our brains forms an intricate pattern of interrelationships with every single sensation and impression. Every new fact, every new experience, immediately sets forth a pattern of growth that spreads like a web to link it with other related and unrelated facts. The pattern serves much the same purpose as the roadways in a neighborhood, linking every address with another. But in many ways the links are like foot-trodden pathways through fresh territory: the first trip establishes the path, but it is only through use that the path becomes worn enough to be permanent; untended through disuse, the path just as easily disappears into the underbrush again—the new fact remains, but largely inaccessible. We say we "forgot." The more that access and use the new information or mental ability, the more established the pattern of connections becomes, effectively building the initial path into a well-traveled and permanent roadway within our brains. This development happens with, and only through, stimulation.

Studies have shown that an infant born with a cataract, a rare occurrence, will remain permanently blinded within as little as six months if the growth is not removed. An adult with a similar ailment can easily regain clear and full vision through surgery even if the cataract is left in place for much longer. The reason, the scientists say, is that we must all "learn" to see. Not using the ability from birth prevents us from developing this capacity, even if any physical restriction is later removed. The interconnections allowing vision remain forever unformed, despite surgery.

This gives us an insight into the functioning of that vast, untapped 90 percent of our brains. Because, from birth, we are encouraged to express ourselves with spoken and written words or through touch—limiting our acceptable and reliable inputs and outputs to those that we can express through the five senses—we progressively limit our capacity to receive or transmit information with any other sense. In effect, we remain "blinded" because we have never allowed ourselves to see.

In the course of his extensive and exhaustive studies into the workings of the mind, the psychologist Carl Jung came to the conclusion that we each are born with a highly developed brain filled with the "psychic functioning of the whole human race," connected from birth to what he called "the collective unconscious." He also concluded that "telepathic phenomena are undeniable facts."

As cited in "The Soul and Death ('Seele und Tod')," *Europaische Revue,* in 1934, Jung wrote: "The fact that we are totally unable to imagine a form of existence without space and time by no means proves that such an existence is in itself impossible."

More than fifty years of observation and personal experience drove Jung to believe that a "transpsychic reality" hovered immediately beyond our psychologically accepted psyche. But the exact nature and capacity of this region of ability stretches far beyond our limited understanding and "contains as many riddles as the universe."

What he was saying remains true: our insistence that something is not possible does not make it so, but it certainly limits our capacity to recognize it.

Developing theories of the workings of the brain also indicate that our intelligence is innate and develops through a series of specific unfolding stages, each opening the way to a new level of intelligence. We may ladle in buckets of information and facts, so-called knowledge, but the development of intelligence continues at its own pace. The knowledge gained through both personal and shared experience is necessary, of course, because without it our brains remain like incredibly powerful computers, idling along with no data to compute. But intelligence— and higher intelligence—evolves through a series of opening doors leading to ever higher planes.

The children born now under the dramatic and increasing influence of Aquarius come to us with expanded powers, but if we do not listen to and encourage them, their capacities will atrophy. As with the muscles of our body, failure to exercise our powers limits the growth of those powers. A child kept in a seat will never learn to walk, a child hindered from running will never gain speed and endurance. Similarly, a child constantly told that what he sees are just meaningless dreams or daydreams, constantly told that such-and-such is impossible, will never reach the limits of his vision or reach beyond what is believed possible.

Someone once asked Albert Einstein the secret to making discoveries. "When all the scientists present have agreed that something is impossible," he replied, "one arrives late for their meeting and solves the impossible."

The children arriving now have no conception of what is or is not impossible. That makes them especially well suited to lead us beyond the limits of what we believe to be possible, into whole new realms.

In this way, our children are our teachers as much as our students, especially now. It is said that children choose their parents as they come into this world from a state of unity with the universal spirit, returning to this plane at exactly the place, at exactly the precise moment, and with exactly the people they want or should be with. They come to teach and to learn. Denying them the chance to do so limits the chances of their completing the lesson they came for, as well as limiting the chances of our learning ours.

The powers of mind that until now seemed accessible only to a few are now within the reach of every child. Every child born now has the ability to see deep into the future and the past. It is simply a matter of letting themselves see. The influence of the age is already opening the door for the children to see what can be. They come at this very moment because they are supposed to. They come because they are supposed to help guide us into the New Millennium and guide us beyond it.

If we reject their visions, condemn them for their dreams, we are sealing them off from the universal spirit—and we are sealing ourselves off, as well.

Psychological stress and shock, researchers have noted, cause biological changes within our brains and can permanently close off certain areas of development or force us into recurring patterns of thought, even to the point of constantly dredging up painful recurring memories that we find impossible to leave behind. Physical or psychological abuse, even a painful loss or accident, causes permanent scars that can cripple the mind's development just as catastrophically as a serious injury can permanently impair the development of our limbs.

Parenting, then, is much more than just a biological and economic responsibility. It is a spiritual and emotional responsibility. And it is a two-way street.

But these children of today already exhibit not just the expanded mental powers that will be considered commonplace in the New Millennium, they also demonstrate the raging individuality, independence, and desire for unity that characterize the New Age.

The rebelliousness of youth that we are witnessing—in music and dress and in ways of thinking—is but the manifestation of that desire to prove for themselves everything that is worth knowing. Rebellion symbolizes their desire for change. They are saturated with the energy that tells them that humanity cannot continue as it has. That energy may show itself negatively, even in violence, but that is only because they don't know how to channel it yet. Their time is now and our role is to help them. The challenge for each of us who are already adults, parents or not, is to allow the children who are now coming into the world to exercise their minds and free will without having to fight through the preconceptions we impose on them.

Youths already see the world around them differently from the way older generations do. They do not recognize national borders as barricades. Music and movies, technology and TV link every one of them to an entire generation that spans the globe. A teenager in Moscow listens to much the same music as a youngster in Chile. No matter in what language the words are sung, the young of the world hear the meaning of the song. They recognize far better than older generations that our similarities are much greater than our differences, and they wonder why the rest of humanity can't see it as well.

Aleksandr Kwasniewski, Poland's president, said in an interview at the start of 1996 that he could see the difference in the way his own teenage daughters looked at the world. "They use computers," he said. "They surf the Net. They watch CNN and Eurosport. They love MTV."

His daughters, Kwasniewski said, treated all the debate over whether or not to enlarge the NATO alliance as the pointless chatter of bureaucrats. The young of the world, they told him, "have enlarged many times over; we are united around the world."

And in his daughters' words, Kwasniewski said he learned a lesson: "That is our challenge now and our responsibility. We have to realize that the generations already coming up see far wider than us politicians: that MTV is more important than NATO."

The New World order was but a necessary prelude to a New World, one in which borders don't exist. The young already see that New World, a "global village" in which our common desires and goals far outweigh the individual interests of a single government. The young revel in their individuality and independence while recognizing their unity with all others on this planet.

Naturally, children have always been or at least seemed rebellious, dissatisfied with the ways of their parents. But now it is even more so. Now they are permeated with the power of the New Age, which in itself promotes revolutionary change.

The Aquarian influence, as I have already stated, stretches back for decades. The children of the sixties, the famous flower children who banded together in an unprecedented revolutionary challenge of their parents' status quo, exhibited the tremendous impact of that Aquarian energy. Their goals, in their essence, were distinctly Aquarian: peace, love, understanding. Everything from their music to their form of dress was a departure, a way of being different, of breaking free. And they proclaimed it loudly in the style and the words of their music when they sang that it was, in fact, "the dawning of the Age of Aquarius."

The youth of the sixties challenged the existing mores and beliefs that they were brought up to uphold. They were the natural founders of our current environmental movements as they insistently condemned the destruction of the planet. And they were the inventors and advocates of the technological development most capable of continuing the linking of humanity around the globe: the personal computer.

That the movement temporarily ended owes more to the fact that it accomplished its primary goal than to any failure of the generation that promoted it. The rebellious youth of the sixties united principally to oppose the war in Vietnam. When the war ended in 1975, so did most of the movement. Its influence remained, of course, but with no primary purpose to unite them, the masses that had banded together through the mid- to late-1960s dispersed. The youths went on with their lives, on to bring another generation into the world.

But despite the affirmations and proclamations of the revolutionary young of the sixties, it is their children and their younger siblings who are truly the children of Aquarius.

The generation immediately following the so-called baby boomers carries a number of names. They have been called the baby bust generation, which many of them reject because the title defines them only in terms of their predecessors. Some, considering them to be somewhat disillusioned seekers, have termed them the new lost generation, which once again denies them an identity of their own and defines them only in terms of the first group to bear the name "lost generation," back in the 1920s.

Author Geoffrey T. Holtz, in his book *Welcome to the Jungle*, made an argument that they should be called the "free genera-tion." This group, born in the sixties through about 1980, he wrote, is liberated and emancipated in the sense that the world offered them more options than those open to any preceding generation. They also are *free* in the sense of extra or spare, Holtz wrote, because they felt themselves to be thought of as somewhat superfluous to the rest of society. But, he continued, they also are "free spirits" who lived more uninhibited, more carefree, and, even, more reckless lives than their predecessors.

Despite the many appellations and their various merits as such, novelist Douglas Coupland coined the most common des-ignation: generation X, using the mathematical symbol for the unknown, because these youths resent and defy definition and classification.

By any name, members of this generation make up the teenagers and "twentysomethings" who define youth culture around the world. They are the inventors of the modes of dress and music that exert the influences shaping fashion and artistic trends into today's pop culture. And their collective behavior is redefining the way the world perceives itself—as the Polish president, Kwasniewski, recognized.

In practically every realm, this generation that defies classifi-cation exhibits its individuality. In the area of music alone, they have added hip-hop, grunge, rap, gangsta rap, techno-rave, and funk-rap fusion. Their fashions have nostalgically repopularized the miniskirt and hip huggers, but they defiantly don them with combat boots and have nihilistically adopted body piercing as a generational choice of adornment. They exude new and independent forms of expression even in the bold colors of their makeup.

Seeing them, it becomes obvious that as much as they resent and resist classification, this new generation defines itself with its Aquarian independence. They are united in their rejection of the unquestioning acceptance of the status quo and in their anticipation of everything that is new. And it is obvious from their behavior that they are not just rebellious for its own sake, but because they are seekers in search of a new way that they will call their own.

Now they too are becoming parents. And their children will be much more of everything they are and of everything they are not. The children being born now at the brink of the New Millennium, born to the generation Xers and the baby boomers, are doubly influenced. They are imbued by the spirit of independence and individuality inherited from their parents, saturated by the growing potency of the energy of the age. That they too should be full of revolutionary ideas and rebellious ways is only fitting. It is their birthright as the children of the New Age. It is up to their parents to recognize them as such.

All these factors together make parenting in the New Age different from what it was in the past. Not too long ago, children were expected to follow in their parents' footsteps. This still happens in many parts of the world. If the grandfather was a shoemaker, the son had to be a shoemaker, and the grandson as well. We followed family traditions. It had nothing to do with anyone's personal affinities, qualities, or desires. It was an obligation. The New Age is the age of individuality, a time when everyone can fly freely. It will no longer cause anyone any pain for the child of a doctor to be a pilot, or a dancer, or anything he or she wants to be. The custom of respecting the traditions of the parents is done away with completely.

Also in the not too distant past, other parents who saw themselves as enlightened did not force their children to follow a family tradition, but they exerted just as much influence over their children's final decision as if they had. Call it the "My son, the doctor" syndrome. Parents, thinking they benefited their children in this way, pushed them toward specific aspirations. Driven by what they considered good intentions, they gently, or not so gently, closed off certain avenues and opened specific ones. They coerced with words and actions and even simple signs of approval or disapproval. They tried to make their children better than what they had been, to make them extensions of their own lives or of their failed dreams. From the earliest possible moment, they planted the idea of what a child was to grow to be. "You have to do well in science if you're going to be a doctor," they would say. Or they would give a play doctor's bag for a birthday gift. The directing litany played itself out in every possible instance. "We've had to struggle and work hard all of our lives. But you'll have it much better as a ..."

Now is the time for parents to let their children discover and choose what they want to do with their lives. But they must be allowed to discover it. That means that our educational systems will have to follow the lead of the parents and let children take the time to pursue their own interests. Thomas Edison was encouraged to investigate the things he was curious about. What would have happened if he had not been encouraged? What would have happened if Mozart's family had insisted that he be a doctor or a lawyer?

In the New Millennium, children must be allowed to determine their own paths through life. They must be allowed to find their own inclinations and their own individual talents. Every one of us knows in our hearts and in our souls what it is that we are best suited for and what we enjoy doing the most. In times of crisis, we see people assuming their natural roles. When order has fallen to chaos around them because of an earthquake or a hurricane, people naturally reach for what they are best suited to do. Lawyers don't insist on writing briefs—one will grab a hammer, another will bring a stretcher.

We each have our own special mission in life, and if we let ourselves we can each find our way to do just that. Our children are no different. We need to let them. We can guide them, help them, and offer them alternatives. But every child must find his or her own preferences. Then, it is our place to assist them in making the most that they can of themselves with that preference.

That also involves being able to let go of our children. We are responsible for them when they are too young to care for themselves. We are responsible for feeding them, dressing them, and for opening the way for them to find and choose their own path in life. But we cannot hold on to them or restrict them. Birds leave the nest when they are ready to fly. They go where they want to then, on their own wings. Our children are the same.

To help them find the right path, we must serve as more than guides. We must serve as examples, for we are guides whether we want to be or not. Children learn by example. If we come home from work full of bitterness and anger, full of frustration and harshness, that is what our children will learn. Children copy what they see. They mimic, they absorb. Whatever behavior is shown to them, they will adopt as their own, even if later in life they must fight to discard that behavior. So we must be role models in every way.

That doesn't mean that children must be surrounded by all the comforts of life, showered with gifts, or live in luxury. Their house does not have to be a palace, just a home. Nor do parents have to be perfect, just human. They have to be there when their children want to talk and play and ask questions. A simple touch when a child has fallen has as much power as all the words in the world. It is part of the spontaneous lessons of life that spring from the soul.

The New Millennium brings with it a rebirth of spirituality. The children of the New Age will find themselves naturally drawn to the spiritual, and again we need to open the alternatives to them so that they may discover what is their own personal and best way. Imposing a religion on a child, expecting them to follow any single path is as detrimental to them and to us as forcing them into a specific career field. Religion itself is in the process of undergoing dramatic and everlasting change. Decisions about religion need to undergo similar change. Whether you have rejected existing forms of organized religion or remain firmly attached to one does not mean that your children must, or should even, necessarily adopt the same.

Some children—even though they are suffused with a spirit of independence and individuality that will make their interpretations of religious teachings highly personal—may choose what we may think of as an extremely traditional, even rigid, religion. There is a reason. Let them experiment. Let them learn. Let them make their own choices about the path to God and enlightenment.

Does New Age parenting, or the parenting style of the New Millennium, mean that parents are supposed to just stand back and allow their children to do whatever they want? Of course not. Just as you would not allow your child to touch a hot stove and get burned just so that he or she can know the experience, you should not let your child wander aimlessly through life without guidance and help. A child learns to walk by holding on to things, lifting himself or herself up, and taking tentative steps; sometimes we let them hold our hands as they take the steps that lead them across a room to reach a place they could not walk to on their own; so too with the lessons of life that we can share with our children.

Our mission once we become parents is to assist and to guide—but not to shackle. Once children learn to walk, we will not let them just wander off on their own, to step in front of cars or off high ledges. Someday we must be prepared to follow our children when they lead us and allow them the chance to lead us to someplace we have never been before.

# 11

## Preparing Yourself for the New Millennium—Now

The change of ages comes whether we want it to or not, whether we are prepared for it or not. As the New Millennium arrives, it spreads its mantle of energy over all of us equally, demanding that we abandon the old ways of society and self and adopt the new. Those who resist its influence will be caught in turmoil, tossed in turbulence as they see their world changing and feel themselves helpless to stop that change. The rest of us will find ourselves swept up by the current of the times, drawn rushing into the spirit of the golden age.

But even those of us who welcome the new era can find ourselves feeling as though we are reeling, rushing out of control in a tempest of change instead of flowing smoothly and easily with the spirit of Aquarius. It's up to you. You can sit back and wait to be swept along like a cork on swift white water or you can prepare for the change, open yourself to it by breaking free of the programming of the past, now.

Our programming comes to us millions of times in millions of different ways. It comes from the time of our births and builds day by day throughout our lives. The foundation is laid even before we understand the words that are its bricks, long before they are built one upon another into the immense walls that imprison us. It begins with disapproving looks and with frowns; it grows when we are not nurtured when we cry.

But the bricks and the mortar that make the walls most solid are built of that simple word "no." With that word, we let ourselves be judged. With it, we learn to judge ourselves and others. Because at the root of every disapproving thought, at the base of every expression of distaste, at the heart of every instance of intolerance, is that very first no we ever heard.

Two simple but immensely powerful thoughts guide our every action, or inaction, from birth: fear of rejection and fear of punishment. No is the verbal expression we associate with those fears, the trigger that releases a lifetime of collected impressions. No came before we were set in the corner, ordered to bed, or swatted by an angry hand. No came before someone turned their back on us. Together, no and our reaction to our fears build into the basis for our ideas of good and bad, right and wrong. "No, don't do that." "No, stop that." "No, that's wrong." "No, they are different." No is leveled in judgment and leveled in punishment. We learn, "No! Bad boy!" and its opposite, "Yes. Good girl."

The system is enhanced as the years go on. In school, there are levels of good and bad, from A to F, but it only serves to enhance the idea of being judged by others, of seeking approval. The fear of disapproval, the fear of rejection, the fear of punishment, the fear of hearing no, undermines our ability to decide for ourselves and to learn for ourselves. Fear closes us off from ourselves by turning us outward, looking without instead of within for approval, for fulfillment, for value.

Piece by piece, day by day, we internalize the judgments and the punishments, turning them, day by day, into our own. They become the internal arbiter over our every thought and action, causing us to reflect on the result before we do anything. At their worst, they paralyze us with fear, immobilizing us into inaction. Even when we think we are deciding for ourselves, too often it is that internal voice directing us with the simple question, "Will they like me if I do that?"

The eroding power of fear can destroy our capacity for self-realization; at its worst, it can destroy our sense of self-worth. When we constantly seek for others to value what we do, we too often lose our own ability to place value on ourselves. Eventually, rather than doing the right thing because it is what we want to do, we do the thing that those around us want us to do. Link by link we make our own chains.

Machiavelli would say that this is the perfect example of the end justifying the means. He would say that if we do good because we are afraid of what will happen if we don't, then we do good nonetheless. But that form of thinking is probably the very reason that Machiavelli's name has become synonymous with ruthless disregard for others and his form of reasoning has become the justification for all those who impose their will on others. The difference between Machiavelli's Piscean thinking and the thinking of the New Age is the difference between breathing to stay alive and taking a deep breath to enjoy the crisp freshness of the air. It is the difference between being forced to swim from a sinking boat and swimming for the sheer pleasure of feeling the water gliding over us, of reveling in the power of our muscles to pull us smoothly through the water. It is the difference between being chained and being free, the difference between misery and liberty.

Fear freezes us and we wind up living in the earthly equivalent of the seventh circle in Dante's *Inferno*, locking out the splendor of life itself, locking ourselves in ice.

Skillful manipulators know the value of our fear and how to use it as a weapon against us. Sadly, too many of us allow ourselves to become willing slaves, submitting to the demands and dictates of others in hopes of being liked—or, at least, hoping we won't be punished. We are victims of our own fear, and we have delivered the power of that fear into the hands of others to be used against us. Through fear, preachers and politicians have controlled us, cowed us, tormented us.

Rather than accepting the fact that God truly loves each and every one of us for ourselves, for who we are, we let ourselves believe in a fearsome God, a threatening God who eagerly rains fire and damnation down on those of us who do not strictly adhere to the rules imposed by our prelates. They pump us full of fear of hell and the devil, rather than with a love of heaven and God.

In this view, God forever lies outside us and we must seek grace. In this view, innocent children are born bearing the burden of the original sin, condemned until they can atone, guilty until proven innocent again; at birth, we are marked with a dark stain that we must spend our lives cleansing to remove. But on its face this is absurd. How can a wonderful newborn in all of his or her brilliant purity be a sinner? Would God, the same one the Bible says "is love," permit this? When a newborn infant tragically dies shortly after birth, is that baby really doomed to perdition or, at best, purgatory; yet somehow, once infants are baptized in a ceremony that no baby could possibly understand, suddenly they are granted admittance to Heaven?

No, we are not born stained by original sin; we are born brilliant with the original blessing. We are born full of the divine spark of life, and it is the stain of fear that clouds our view of that eternal beauty and slowly seals us off from the universal spirit. We are born full of limitless possibilities, and the limits are imposed as we grow.

Politicians pour out propaganda designed to make us believe in monsters and victims. Their speeches are filled with the theme of values and of protecting our values. But are they really talking about *our* values? Or are they really talking about their values and including the rest of us because they know that since so many of us are looking to others to tell us what to do, we'll allow them to tell us what our values are?

Sharing the same values as others is not wrong. Because of all that we share in common, it is natural that we hold many of our values in common as well. But each of us must decide for ourselves what those values are. If we allow ourselves to be indoctrinated by others, if we do not look inside ourselves, we cannot see for ourselves what is of value. Blindly accepting the values of others based on faith is contrary to the spirit of the New Age. In the New Millennium, we go beyond faith to find knowledge. We may come away believing exactly as we do now, but we know it for ourselves, not because someone else told us it is so.

In the Age of Aquarius, what is important is to know, not just to blindly believe.

When you go to buy a car, you turn on the engine, you drive it a little bit, and you look under the hood to see if it's in good condition—to see if it's a good *value* for the price. Yet when we are talking about something so important as our own souls, something so vital as our own salvation, we accept when we are told that we can't examine too closely. That in itself should be a warning. Not everyone who claims to have an answer really does. If they truly know, they'll be able to answer your questions.

We must be extremely careful when picking what door to knock on or what master to listen to in the matters of God and spirituality. Anyone who tries to make you dependent or tries to fill you full of fears—fears of punishments or fear of a distant and cruel God—should not be heeded. God's desire is that we all live in happiness and peace and it is through love that we find our way to the light and join with the universal spirit.

But very few gurus and preachers truly want us to find our own way to God. Very few want us to learn the divine truth because if we do, we won't need them. Someone who truly knows that we are each entitled to become one with God, who knows that heaven is in our hearts and in our souls, is happy for us to discover this for ourselves. People who truly know the way of the universe know that when we reach the point of truth and join with the cosmic consciousness, we join more totally with them as well. The ones who wish to remain our paid interpreters of knowledge fear losing their position, so they turn our fear against us, threatening that if we don't follow their way, we won't find salvation. They insist on being our go-betweens with God instead of our guides on the spiritual path.

Of course, it is not just in spiritual matters that we allow fear to dominate us. In almost everything we do, fear becomes our motivator, from without and from within. We fear losing our jobs, so we put up with dictatorial bosses; we fear losing our freedom, so we put up with dictatorial rulers. These are very real fears indeed, but we even look for love out of fear. We seek love out of our fear of being alone instead of finding love for its own sake. We believe that if someone else loves us, then we are lovable. Love from outside of us takes the place of us loving ourselves. We go in search of approval rather than fulfillment.

And to what lengths we'll go to find that approval! We act the way we think others want us to be, losing sight of ourselves. We act self-consciously, or we don masks, instead of acting naturally and being ourselves. Fearing that the object of our desire will judge us or reject us, we try to shape ourselves to what we think they want us to be. We pose; we posture; we primp—all without ever letting the other see who we really are.

If we succeed in attracting that person, we let them control us through the fear that if we let our guard down, they will leave us. We have set the trap, stepped into the vicious circle for ourselves. Wanting to be loved, we acted like someone we are not; finding someone and ending up in a relationship forces us to continue the act, because they never really loved us for who we really are. How could they? They never knew us to begin with. They only knew the person we let them see, the one we wanted them to see, so that they would love us. And through it all, we feel tremendously empty, but are unable to put our finger on the reason why. We may go through an entire lifetime in a relationship that leaves us lacking, because we looked for love outside of ourselves instead of beginning by loving ourselves.

All because we seek approval from others; because we seek our values—even our value of ourselves—from others; all because we fear rejection, fear being alone. Fear becomes our shackle in love, and in life.

Some who already have felt the influence of Aquarius but who are still deluded by the influence of Pisces go to others to teach them how to find themselves. By successfully completing the courses taught by these self-appointed swamis, they receive a certificate or a diploma that says, in effect, that they are now enlightened. But the diploma is nothing more than a seal of approval. The students go in search of wisdom, or at least go thinking that they are searching for wisdom, and come away satisfied by receiving approval from a so-called master. In fact, they are just as lost as before. But they avoided rejection and won approval, and that, for many, is just as good.

If you truly wish to find wisdom then learn this: no one can teach you anything! They may show you what they know or help you find the way, but you must learn for yourself. The awakening comes from within yourself, and *only* from within yourself.

Still, one popular thing for people to try nowadays on these voyages of self-realization is fire walking. They go to seminars and take classes in the art of walking barefoot across hot coals. The goal, of course, is to cross without burning their feet. And, they are led to believe, if they can accomplish that then they will become self-actualized—whatever that means. But the whole ritual of walking on fire is not about walking on fire, it is about overcoming, of defeating, your fear. And you don't have to walk on fire to do that. Christ walked on water; people pay to walk on fire; in the New Millennium, we will walk on air. By breaking free of your fear and believing in yourself, by letting yourself connect to the universal oneness, you will not sink, you will not burn, you will not fall—you will fly.

That is the lesson of the New Age. That is the lesson God wants us all to learn. But it begins by looking inside ourselves, not by looking to someone else for the answers. You don't have to compare yourself to anyone. You don't need anyone's approval. You need to look for your own inner light. That is enlightenment. You need to discover and develop your own individuality, your own divine uniqueness, your own divinity. That is how we find our way back to the oneness of the universe.

It may sound sacrilegious, but we are all gods in our own way. We all carry a part of the divine spark within us. In the beginning, astronomers tell us, the entire universe exploded out from a single, infinitesimally tiny point. Everything in the universe since comes from that same single burst of energy. The stars, the planets, us—everything—began from the same substance.

Think of that energy, that substance, as a beautiful diamond. At the moment that it burst outward, it sent tiny fragments of itself flying out—to become the seed for everything that came afterward. That "star seed," that essence, that brilliant bit of diamond, still glows within each of us and within everything in the universe.

If that beautiful diamond is what we think of as the divinity, the creator of all things, then we each are a part of the divinity, carrying within us the spark of the divine.

Recognizing that, we come closer to God and closer to uniting once again with the divine spirit of the universe that flows in, around, over, and through everything in the cosmos. Recognizing that we carry the divine spark within us allows us to flow more freely into the great cosmic current. Rather than remaining apart from God, we become one with God and immediately begin to bring divine love, peace, and harmony into our lives.

The Bible speaks of the Second Coming of Christ. But that doesn't necessarily mean that Christ will step down physically onto the Earth again, white robe and all. It means that the spirit of Christ, the Christian ideal, reigns on Earth. That happens when we each discover our own cosmic, inner Christ. The golden millennium begins with our individual awakening to the Christ that is within each of us, when we realize we are all the children of God, eternally and marvelously connected to the divine source.

We are divine and immortal. We come from that divine source, we remain part of it, and we return to it when we leave this body.

In his *Arcano Coelestia*, Emanuel Swedenborg, the Swedish mathematician and mystic, put it this way: "It can in no sense be said that heaven is outside of any one; it is within ... and a man also, so far as he receives heaven, is a recipient, a heaven, and an angel."

Realizing that frees us from our fears. We cannot even fear death when we know that we go on for all eternity. We cannot fear rejection when we know that we are divine, in our own way, and part of the divinity. But to reach that realization we must go within, further than we ever have. It is only within ourselves that we will discover the absolute truth, the one truth.

We can begin that voyage to our innermost selves by opening ourselves to the spirit of the New Millennium. We can begin by planting the thoughts that reverse our programming. As you sow, so shall you reap. You can begin to undo your programming this instant with thoughts of love and prosperity, which is what God truly wishes for all of us. Aquarius is the age of plenty for all. We are all equally interconnected to the universal spirit, so it is impossible that some of us would be more deserving than others. All of us are entitled to prosperity and well-being, if we choose, and all of us are entitled to love.

Thinking those thoughts, recognizing that you are part of the universal order with every right to share all of its beauty, opens you to the spirit of Aquarius and prepares you to enter the New Millennium, ready to savor its fruits.

Of course, our programming was not all suddenly heaped on us. We did not suddenly wake up one morning desperate for approval. So you shouldn't be disappointed when you can't suddenly undo a lifetime's worth of programming in a single sitting. But by chipping away at the base of our programming, by chiseling steadily at the foundation of fear that limits us, we can bring the walls crumbling down much faster than it took to put them up. By taking away the fear, we take the power of our fear away from those who would use it against us. By taking away the fear, we free ourselves to think for ourselves, without worrying about what others think. If I don't fear your rejection, I don't need your approval; if I don't need your approval, I am free to decide for myself—and I am free to be me.

In the New Millennium we are all free to be ourselves. We can take off our masks and be natural. Being natural means being like things are in nature, in their natural state. In nature, animals don't try to be like other animals. A cat doesn't try to be a dog, and a dog doesn't try to fly like a bird. Why should we be any different? Why should you want to wear the clothes that everyone else is wearing if you don't like the way they look on you? Why should you always hide your face behind makeup and lipstick? When you want to, go ahead. A proud peacock sometimes shows off all of its bright feathers. But sometimes it doesn't. It does what comes naturally, and so should we.

What matters is what is inside. That is where our true beauty lies. That is where we will connect with the universe. We don't reach out and touch the universal spirit with our hands. We can touch its material manifestations—a flower, a feather, a snowflake—with our material manifestation of its spirit, our hands. But touching the cosmic consciousness itself is done with our consciousness, with our hearts and our souls.

Naturally, none of us is perfect; and while that doesn't make us any less deserving of being loved for who and what we are, neither should we be satisfied being anything less than we can be. To truly reach into your inner self, you must peel away the protective layers of a lifetime of defenses and rationalizations. To see your essence, you must know your essence. And there may be some things you see that you don't like. That's okay. But it's not okay to just shrug your shoulders and leave it that way. The law of karma says that if we don't learn our lessons in this lifetime, we will have to repeat the lessons until we do. The cycle ends not just because we recognize our connection to the divine spirit, but because we have learned to emulate the divine ideals. Putting it simply: to be of the one, you're supposed to act like it. Luckily for us all, we are now blessed by the power of Aquarius, and we can go further in this single lifetime than we ever have before.

The essence of the universal spirit is love. It is complete, all-encompassing, total, true love. In account after account, people who have had near-death experiences, those who died on the operating table only to come back to life minutes later, always describe the same two sensations. One, they see an intensely bright light that drew them toward it; and two, they describe an incredible feeling of total love, of peace. The feeling of love is so overwhelmingly powerful that many who come back after knowing it cry for days, wondering why they had to return to life rather than being allowed to stay with it. That love is the essence of the divinity, of the universal spirit. But you don't have to die to know it. You can connect to it in life, but you must be saturated with the same feeling; and the only way to know true love is to begin by loving yourself. That for many of us will be the most difficult challenge of all.

We have a lifetime of negative affirmations that we shoulder everywhere we go. We have thousands, millions, of reasons to believe we are not worthy. We grade ourselves, rate ourselves, constantly; and, constantly, we judge ourselves unworthy. Just as we can make ourselves sick by constantly planting negative thoughts in our minds, so can we make ourselves unworthy of love. "He'd never go out with someone like me," we say. "She wouldn't be interested in me." What we are really saying is, "I don't love me. How could they?" But we are all equally worthy of being loved if we choose to be.

To love ourselves, we must begin by truly examining ourselves. Start by listing your negative traits, the things you don't like about yourself. It's okay, we all have some. But we are speaking of matters of the soul now, not of the body. So you must separate between the negative physical flaws on your list and the negative spiritual things. We almost always start off lists of this sort with things such as, "I'm too fat," or "I'm too skinny." Sometimes, the negative traits on our list have to do with our habits: "I smoke too much," or "I'm sloppy." But all of these things are physical in nature, not spiritual.

Finding our real character flaws is much more difficult. Even what most of us think of as our inner flaws are still inner perceptions of our outer being. "I lack self-control," say the people who really mean that they think they eat too much and, because of that, they are too fat. "I'm too indecisive," say the people who really mean that they hesitate before taking physical action because they are still controlled by their fears. But these are not yet real character or spiritual flaws; they are merely the internalizations of physical manifestations.

Our spiritual flaws are much harder to find and define, because the truth is most of us aren't as flawed as we make ourselves believe. Did you mock a physically disabled person? That is a flaw of character. Did you take pleasure in someone else's misfortune? Even if they deserved it, that is a flaw. Did you hate? Were you intolerant? Are you easy to anger? Those are character traits, spiritual flaws, that you must work to correct.

But should you love yourself less because of those traits? No! Of course not. They are part of your totality, part of your essence, and by recognizing them as flaws and working to correct them, you are announcing that you wish to perfect yourself, to learn your lesson, and to join with the universal oneness. But you don't have to dislike yourself because of them. By making peace with your internal demons, those negative aspects of your character, you make peace with yourself; and by making peace with yourself, you begin to love yourself.

Once you love yourself, you begin to reach toward that universal feeling of love. Once you love yourself, you can truly love others. Once you love yourself, you will look at your life differently and others will look at you differently. Your inner beauty, all the wonderful things about you that have been hidden by the layers of doubt and fear burst out from you, radiating from every pore—you'll glow. And others will see that glow and recognize your true beauty. You've probably already met some people like that, people who exude a certain, seemingly undefinable *something*; people with a certain *magnetism*. They may not necessarily be attractive in the traditional, physical definition, but they are always invited to parties and on dinner dates, and they seem equally comfortable in a five-star restaurant as in the middle of a field looking up at the clouds. Ask them about it and invariably, at first at least, they'll smile with a look that says, "Thanks, but I don't know what you're talking about." But look closely, in their smiling eyes, you'll see that they do indeed *know* ... something.

What they know is what you can learn: they know peace; they know they can love themselves; they know they can be comfortable being natural without any masks.

Which is not to say their life is a bed of roses. Every living person has, has had, and will have problems. But no one should let their problems make them bitter. Too often, our problems come from within us. We manufacture our problems in our minds, in our well of fears and insecurities, and through constant reinforcement they take real form in the physical world. We bring them into being with the power of our will. But we hardly ever think that we can make them disappear in the same way. Those people who do *know*, the ones who seem so comfortable, the ones who are at peace, know this as well. They see their problems as challenges or experiences; they see them as lessons to be learned. They continue to love themselves, continue to think positively about themselves and about life, and remain at peace as they study their situation. They lose their jobs, even, but they continue to think that there must be a reason, that they must be intended for something better. While they are looking for that new job, they come closer to their families, spending more time with their spouses and children. They realize that they need more balance in their lives, time for both their jobs and their families. They learn a positive lesson. And soon enough, they have an even better job than they had before.

We look at those people and shake our heads. We say, "You always seem to land on your feet." But the truth is that they land on their feet because they expect to. They are just like experienced gymnasts who fly free of the parallel bar, twirl through a complicated maneuver, and land nimbly upright. The gymnast has practiced the move enough to where she expects to land on her feet and does. You have practiced living all of your life; if you expect to land on your feet, you will.

Every day that goes by is lost. It can never be replaced. Every day of living the way you are keeps you from living the way you can. The sooner you journey deep within yourself and let yourself see the true beauty that is there, the sooner you allow that beauty to come out for others to see, and the sooner beautiful things will begin to happen to you.

The further you go, the closer you will come into contact with the spirit guides who will show you the way. Call them angels, nature spirits, visions, or voices, but they will come to speak to you in your tranquillity and to light the way to your individual illumination. Even if you think of them only as your inner voice, you will hear, and feel, and know that you are on the right path to step confidently and happily into the New Millennium and to help bring peace and love to the world.

# 12

# No Mistakes, No Accidents, No Limits

To live is to learn. That is why you are here: to learn. That is why we continue to return to this terrestrial plane, trying over and over again, getting chance after chance, to learn our lessons—to get it right. We must learn to be compassionate and to live in peace and harmony. We must learn to truly love. But the ultimate lesson that we all are supposed to learn is that we are supposed to live our lives to the fullest. We are supposed to learn to live. And to truly live, we must experiment with life. We need to taste of all of it so that we can savor it in all of its splendor.

The punishment of prison is that it takes people away from the world. Ask prisoners about their life in a cell and what they miss the most. Frequently, they say they miss such things as fishing or walking barefoot across a sandy beach. Quite simple things, fishing and walking on beaches, but they are the essence of living.

For a while, it was quite popular for people to pay a lot of money to be isolated in things called sensory deprivation tanks. These were soundproof, completely dark tanks that people would be locked into, often naked, to be left floating in liquid at their precise body temperature so that not even the sense of touch remained. People would emerge from these tanks in tears, crying for joy, saying they had seen God. Perhaps some did, but too many, I think, missed the point. They emerged thinking that God could only be found inside the tank. And that is where they left their God instead of carrying that sense of divinity with them everywhere they went afterward. When they felt they had lost touch with that divinity, with the meaning of life, they returned to the tank to seek God anew. But the point was not the deprivation, so much. The point was the flood of sensation that came when a person stepped out of the tank and back into the world. That is where God can be found: in life.

Yet too many of us live in prisons of our own making, depriving ourselves of the real sensations of life. We get up at the same time every weekday morning, drink a cup of coffee exactly like the one we drank yesterday, and look over the morning headlines that also seem so much like yesterday's. Then we take a shower, get dressed in clothes quite similar to what we wore to work yesterday, and head for work along the same route we take every morning. We encounter the usual traffic jam at roughly the same place and when we finally get to work, we park in our regular spot. Work usually goes pretty much as it always does. Then we head home at about the same time, through the same evening traffic jam ... and so on.

"I feel like I'm in a rut," we say. And we're right. We've dug a well-worn path and we follow it faithfully day after day. But we feel too depressed to do anything about it, so we plop in front of the TV set to let the pictures wash over us until it's time to go to sleep. Then we get up the next morning and start all over again.

Or, worse, people lose themselves in drugs or alcohol. They do it to deaden their nerves, even though some of them claim that drugs heighten their experience. They say they feel more alive when they do drugs or alcohol. That's their bodies lying to them. Any drug, whether it is alcohol or marijuana or pills or whatever, serves only to deaden the mind. Drugs distance you from yourself rather than help you connect with your inner self. You're still falling, but your deadened nerves lie to you and you think you're landing on cotton rather than concrete. And every day you continue that way, the hole you are falling into gets deeper. One day, the drugs don't work anymore and you fall for good. Wouldn't it be much better to stop falling altogether and learn to fly? To do that you must truly heighten the experience of life. Climb out of the hole; climb out of the rut.

If you're in a hole or a rut, stop! This instant! Before you go to bed tonight, set your alarm for a few minutes earlier than usual. When you wake up, go outside and watch the Sun come up. It does it every day, but no two sunrises are alike. Let yourself marvel at the wonder of how this great cosmic clock turns in such precise rhythm; at how this magnificent dawn paints the sky with such an incredible palette of orange and red and yellow hues. When you're ready to leave, take a different route to work and let yourself see the houses and the buildings and the trees and the other people getting out to go to work or to school.

Living is not always being fanned by palm leaves as you lie on a beach. Living is life and being *aware* of life—constantly. If you relish life, you will love it; and if you love it, you will cherish it. You will cherish your own and you will cherish it in every living person and thing. That is the grand lesson of life, because if you love and cherish all life, you will be kind and compassionate and caring toward all things.

So it is no mistake that you are here. There are no mistakes. In the magnificent cosmic design everything happens for a reason. Every experience, every event, every moment is a lesson. You are supposed to experience so that you can learn.

Newton's Third Law of Motion is the First Law of the Universe, the law of cause and effect: for every action, there is an equal and opposite reaction. On one level, that is how we learn: every experience causes you to react. If you touch something hot, you feel pain and you pull back. You'll be more careful next time. You learned something. You know it for yourself.

If someone tells you something, or about something, it's not the same as knowing it for yourself. To know something for yourself, you have to experience it for yourself. This doesn't mean that if someone tells you the stove is hot you have to touch it and feel the pain for yourself. If you do that, you didn't learn your lesson the first time you ever got burned.

But to truly know for yourself, you have to experience for yourself. Someone telling you about swimming is not the same as swimming for yourself. You can read all the books in the world about swimming and still not know how to do it. The day you dive in the water to try to swim is the day you know if you know how or not. You either swim or you drown. I could read all the books in the world about cooking but that doesn't mean I can even boil an egg. I may understand the theory behind cooking or swimming or whatever, but until I do it, I don't *know* it.

It's the same with everything in life. No one can describe a sunset in a way that makes you know it for yourself. You have to smell a perfume to know what it smells like. You have to be deeply, profoundly, overwhelmingly in love to know love. Sometimes you will like the smell of the perfume and sometimes you won't. Sometimes, the person you love will find another, and that hurts. But you don't dislike all perfumes just because you smelled one you didn't like; you pick a different perfume. And you don't keep yourself from ever loving again just because of one bad experience. There was a *reason* you were supposed to love that first person, and a *reason* they were supposed to leave. Maybe you needed to show you cared more;

maybe you needed to be less dependent. Whatever it was, there was a reason, and there was a lesson.

If you want to think of some of the things that you do in life, some of the painful experiences, as mistakes, that's all right. It's a word we're used to, even if our definition is wrong. But whether you think of them as mistakes or as experiences, have a lot of them. It's the only way to grow. The toddler who falls, who lands with a thump on the floor, sooner or later learns to walk by him- or herself. But watch carefully and you'll notice that toddlers rarely fall the same way twice. They tumble to the left; they tumble to the right; they teeter, wobble, then plop down. But they hardly ever fall the same way twice. With each fall, they learn something new. So can you. Just don't keep making the same mistakes or having the same painful experiences over and over again. Learn from every one of them. If you don't, you'll hurt yourself; or you'll hurt someone else, which, in cosmic terms, is the same as hurting yourself.

It's the first universal law again: for every action there is an equal and *opposite* reaction. These are spiritual laws, not physical, so the reaction may not be *exactly* the same as the action. If you throw a rock at someone, the rock won't necessarily come back and hit you. But something will, sooner or later. Think of it as the boomerang effect: everything you do affects something which, in turn, affects you. What you decide to do decides the effect. Therefore, just as there are no mistakes, there are no accidents.

For example, there are those who spend their entire lives concentrating, focused on their problems. They can't take the time to live because they are too busy worrying or suffering. Many of these problems are of a recurring nature. They appear to be solved only to surge anew later like weeds in the garden of our lives. If they are psychological problems, people apply superficial therapies without result. When they are not the wounds left by those with whom we came in contact over the course of a lifetime, they are the fears of what we don't understand; or they are the manifestations of those wounds and fears, often resulting in an attitude of renunciation—we surrender to our problems and say, "Why bother, it's always the same." That defeatist attitude turns us into critics and cynics and, whether we want it to or not, it drives people away.

All the frustration or negativity that we carry like a cancer in our hearts reflects itself in the way we judge others and ourselves. It is as if it makes us happy or makes us feel superior to attack, demean, or humiliate others. Anyone who does not do things the way I think they should be done, anyone who threatens my security or my status, must be knocked down—judged. Or we need to knock ourselves down, judge ourselves, and we always do it harshly: "I'm so stupid"; "I can't do anything right."

In this way, we continue to attract more problems. The more we judge, the more likely we are to remain alone; the more alone we feel, the more we complain. The vicious cycle continues. We blame our parents or whoever else we think we can make responsible for our problems and our personal tragedies.

The mind is very capable of justifying. Everything can be justified. Even wars are justified; we permit killing in the name of political and religious ideals. But more often than not, the root of our problems is within ourselves. It is not an accident that we have problems; we bring them on ourselves. By projecting negativity constantly, we attract negativity. In the spiritual realm, *like* things attract.

If you are bitter, you exude that mean spirit. You snap at people or you make derogatory comments to them. They won't like you and they won't want to be around you. They may even be mean to you. But you are still to blame. It is no accident. You caused them to not like you.

If you are angry driving your car and you miss a stop sign and hit another car, people call it an accident. But it's not; you caused it. Even if you leave your house angry in the morning, but you drive carefully, stop at the stop sign, and somebody still hits you—it's still your fault. You were angry, you were negative, and that sentiment reached out like a giant magnet and drew that negative event to you. You brought this accident, this problem, on yourself.

What if you left your house happy and positive and feeling great, and somebody slams into you at the corner? It's still not an accident. There is a reason. You just have to figure out what that reason is. It may be that you were just there to help that other person learn a lesson, and that was your lesson in helping. Or that minor fender bender may have saved your life and, in fact, the person who hit you at the corner did you a huge favor because if you had continued on your way, you would have been run over by a truck. Or it may be something you did or thought, but didn't think was important at the time, so you don't remember.

That is why, in the same way we learned in the past chapter that we need to examine our characters for flaws, we need to analyze our problems. What are your complaints? What do you think would make you eternally happy? What do you need to sacrifice in order to gain that which you have always wanted? What are the real and actual obstacles to making your dreams come true? Write them down and analyze them. Remember that the circumstances are not going to change. Everything you have accumulated in your mind and your heart can't just be covered over and buried, but it can become the fertile soil where you plant the seeds of your new life, free of all those horrible problems.

For people at peace with themselves, for people who are truly happy and creative, every problem is a challenge to help them grow, to help them evolve. Every so-called problem is a lesson, an experience to help them acquire wisdom; no problem can destroy them.

Look at your list of problems. How many can be solved just by changing your way of reacting, by moving, by studying, by preparing yourself better to be able to demand better pay and recognition, by daring to do what it takes to make you happy without harming anyone else? To better your real situation you have to be more sincere, honest, and frank with yourself. You have to stop lying to yourself. You must tear away the veil of fantasy and study the harsh reality.

To live is to have problems. They are the load we bear. They are our lessons to learn, even if the lesson is only that we learn to bear the load. If you had learned all your lessons, you wouldn't be here. If you had learned all your lessons, your cycle of reincarnations would have ended and you would have already joined with the universal spirit.

Even when we are trying to do the right thing, trying to be good, we can cause problems for ourselves. Think about it. How many times, in an effort to be good, have you made yourself a martyr or a victim of someone who wants to take advantage of you? How many times have you felt that your child is wasting his or her life, and that as much as you try to be good, this is your cross to bear? If it causes you pain, if it makes you feel frustrated, it becomes a problem. A problem is something that causes us anguish, something we cannot find a solution for, something that robs us of our sleep and paralyzes us in our life.

But how many people accept their so-called problems, things that for others would be overwhelming, with infinite peace and profound love. By learning to bear their loads, their loads become lighter. By figuring out what the real root of their problems are, they can eliminate them. They can drop the load, dump the cross, and get on with their lives. They can get on with living.

This is your life. No one can live it for you, and you don't have to live it for anyone else. If you see every day as a continuation of the tragedies of yesterday, the moment comes when the burden of negativity will crush you. Every day should be a new debut. Every day, the curtain rises again on a brand new premiere showing. You have never seen *this* day before, it's brand new; why, then, should you treat it like all the others of the past? Enjoy this day as a new and different one, one where you have every right to be happy. This is part of the internal preparation we each have to go through to be ready to allow the spirit of the New Age to flow into us.

We have to allow the fresh, the improvised, the new to come into our lives. We are moving into an era of originality, of fresh ideas, of a new way of living in an all New Millennium. The burden we have carried for two thousand years—the dogmas, the dictates—weighs too much. To be able to fly, to be free, we must let go of the burden. You cannot remain paralyzed in your old ways, in your old life, in your old self. The moment has arrived to take off, to fly to infinity.

If you are wrapped up in your problems, you will block out the positive energy that is rushing in over all of us. You'll be inside yourself with your problems and the spirit of Aquarius will remain outside, swirling around you, and you'll be missing it. If you break free of your problems the spirit will be able to flow into you and saturate you.

Begin by getting to know the joy of living. Experiment with life. A sacred word for the New Millennium is "pleasure." In the Age of Pisces, too many pleasures were seen as sins. If we felt we were enjoying anything *too* much, there had to be something wrong with it or with us. Sex has always been the big one, in this manner of thinking. But what is so wrong with totally enjoying sharing ourselves and our bodies with someone we truly care about? The union of two beings in total love and sincere caring cannot be wrong, for it is the very essence of unity and humanity. It is the very essence of life—not the only one, to be sure, but one nonetheless. It is life and living, and like everything else in life, it brings us closer to knowing our connection to the universe, to the supreme spirit flowing through everything in the universe, to recognizing our own divinity.

In India, it is quite common for someone to say to you, "Excuse me, but would you like to be my God for a while?" When someone else approaches, the person with you will smile happily and say, "I am with my God." It's surprising to hear, to our Western ears, but what they mean is that they know that God is in each of us. When they speak to you, they know they are speaking to God. If they speak in anger, that is what God hears. If they speak with words of love, then that is what God hears.

In the West, we think similarly about speaking in anger or speaking with love, but we have more difficulty recognizing that we are divine beings. We "let the spirit into us" and "we become one with God," yet we never let ourselves see ourselves as divine entities. But we are. We are divine creatures with limitless possibilities if we recognize it and allow ourselves to be. We are unlimited beings in an unlimited world, where everything is possible and nothing is impossible.

There are no accidents. There are no mistakes. There are no limits.

We set the limits for ourselves. We are responsible for everything we do and for everything that happens to us. If we believe that bad things will happen to us, they will. The very power of our thoughts makes them real and makes them happen. And they happen for a reason.

If you think you are not going to get a certain job, when you go to the interview you're uncomfortable. You fidget, you look away, you squirm. You hem and you haw. Generally, you give the impression that you're not very likable, you're lying, or both. It would be incredibly good fortune for you to get the job after a performance like that. Sometimes it happens that people see past all the negative vibes we are putting out and see that we are worth a chance. But whether you do or don't get the job, what's more important is: did you learn your lesson?

It works the same with positive thoughts. You may not win the lottery by sitting down and thinking that you're going to win the lottery. And, then again, you might. But at the very least, if you truly think you're going to win the lottery, you're probably going to smile a lot at the thought. When you greet people you're going to be smiling, so they're going to smile in return. Their smiles make you feel a little better and you smile a bit more … and so on. You may not win the lottery, but you got a wealth of smiles and good cheer; you got rich in a way that may be more important than money, just by thinking you were going to win the lottery. You thought you were going to win and you did. You just didn't win exactly what you had in mind.

To enter fully into the New Millennium, to participate fully in the burst of creativity and originality and humanity and love that it brings with it, we must break free of the limiting chains of our minds. Whatever you believe is possible *is;* if you believe something is impossible, it will be—for you.

Within the universal laws, this could be considered the "What you think is what you get" concept. And, again, the spiritual laws conform to natural laws—in this case, to some of the indications of quantum theory in physics and to what is known as the "anthropic principle." *Anthropic* is derived from Greek, meaning "having to do with man" or humanity. According to the scientific principle bearing the name, the universe exists because we are here to see it. It's not a figment of our imaginations but it does exist in the way it does because we are the ones looking. Some go so far as to suggest that it may exist strictly for that purpose—so that we may observe it. The strong anthropic principle suggests, basically, that that may be why

God created the universe in the first place: just for us. The Bible supports the idea, but it seems awfully egotistical for us to think that we are the reason for everything, considering the vastness of the universe. But the view that it appears the way it does because we are the ones looking seems to be supported by quantum physics.

In quantum theory, there are certain conditions in which it is impossible to know what an electron is doing unless we are watching; when we are not, it's not even theoretically possible to know what it might be up to. In universal laws, the spiritual laws, this is extended: things behave the way they do because of the way we look at them.

In the New Millennium we can learn to listen to our bodies and help heal ourselves; we can heal our planet's wounds; we can reach beyond this world to find life on other worlds; and we can learn to use that untapped 90 percent of our minds. We can do all this and so much more, but we must begin with ourselves. Very few believed that Columbus actually would sail across the ocean and not fall off the edge of the flat Earth. But Columbus was convinced the world was round, so he set sail. He proved himself right and wound up discovering much more than he had expected. He thought he was going to find a new trade route to bring home spices from India. He discovered a whole New World.

The New Millennium is a portal to a time of limitless possibilities. As we cross through into what lies ahead, we will glimpse some of those possibilities. But many, many more remain to be discovered. When Thomas Edison patented the Kinetoscope in 1891, it would have been hard to imagine feature-length movies on laser disks and computer CD-ROMs. As we look at those things today, can we see all that they will lead to? We are entering the age of discovery in every field and on every plane. If we enter it convinced that the old ways are the only way, convinced that the world is flat, we limit what we allow ourselves to discover. And any scientist will tell you that the only way to discover is to experiment. By exploring what is with an open mind, you open yourself to what can be. The key is keeping your mind open.

A scientist who experiments seeking to prove his or her pre-conceived notions runs the risk of tainting the results. Scientists test theories, possibilities, to see if they hold true. But in true scientific method, the experimenters must remain open to the possibility of disproving their theories and, quite possibly, to proving something the scientists never suspected.

It is the same as you experiment in life. What you think will be pleasurable may turn out to be the worst experience of your life, and vice versa. What's important is that you experimented, that you opened yourself to the possibilities and discovered what you would. Whatever you try will not be a mistake or an accident; it will be an experience that will swing open the door to more experiences; and the more experiences you allow your-self, the fewer limits you will set for yourself.

How many people do you know who say they can't dance when what they really mean to say is that they have never tried or that they don't think they are particularly good at it? That is a limiting thought. Rather than allowing themselves to experience dancing every chance they get, they say they can't. And by thinking that way, it's true for them. They can't because they haven't tried and they'll never try because they think they can't. If they try they may discover that they will never be what others consider good dancers but, then again, they may turn out to be what we think of as excellent dancers. Even if they remain what most of us consider to be poor dancers, they can at least learn to enjoy the pleasure of losing themselves in the music, learn to enjoy the pleasure of feeling their bodies in motion. Or they may learn that they just plain don't like dancing. That's okay as well. But by remaining open to the possibilities, by experimenting, they know it for themselves and for certain.

Test, taste, savor life. Not even your circumstances can limit you if you don't let them. Some of the best athletes of our time are confined to wheelchairs. Paraplegics and quadriplegics no longer let their disability limit them. They play basketball, they swim, they race on and off road, they lift weights, they work, and they raise families. They live. Injuries and diseases that just a generation or two ago would have been akin to a prison sentence, sealing their victims off from most of life's opportunities, now are seen as challenges. People who have become paralyzed for whatever reason may not be able to experience life in the same way that others do, but they can still experiment and savor it. That is the positive energy of the New Millennium already at work. And if people with physical challenges can open themselves to it, why can't the ones who have full use of their bodies? If people in wheelchairs can allow the power of their minds to overcome their physical challenges, why can't all of us? They know that it is not their bodies but their minds that can chain them, can limit them. We all should realize the same.

# 13

## Dancing to the Rhythm
## of the Stars

The New Age is bursting with the energy of freedom. Freedom means no limits. It means endless possibilities and endless opportunities. The sooner you set yourself to the task of truly opening yourself to that spirit—the sooner you eliminate your self-imposed limits—the sooner you will be able to fully absorb the energy of the New Millennium. By opening yourself to it, you open yourself to an explosion of creativity, of originality, and of inventiveness.

You have already taken the first steps toward that marvelous goal by starting to chisel away at your programming and your fears, and by experimenting with life. But to complete the process of removing your limitations and opening the way to link with the tremendous current of energy flowing around us, you must learn the meaning of *being*.

If the spirit of the New Age is to flow into you, you must first empty yourself so that you can receive it. To truly be *in* the New Millennium, you must learn to be in the here and now; because if you cannot learn to live in the present, when the future becomes today you will not be able to be totally part of it. The spirit of the New Millennium is not just something to look forward to, it is something to start feeling now. If you are always looking to the future, looking straight ahead for it to come, you will be like a horse with blinders on, never looking around you to realize where you are, and you may not even realize that the Age of Aquarius is already here.

The time comes whether we are ready for it or not. Somewhere beyond the edge of our consciousness, celestial forces play their eternal rhythm in a complex cosmic concert. We are dancers in this cosmic concert, and just like dancers moving to the music of a composition here on the terrestrial plane, we can step in time with the rhythm or stumble awkwardly against it. The more at ease we are with the rhythm, the more naturally and gracefully we flow, learning even to elaborate upon the basic steps, to relish the music and the dancing.

So too with the celestial music that plays constantly around us.

The noted astronomer Johannes Kepler began his intensive studies of astrology in 1600, in an effort to discredit it once and for all. His teacher, Tycho Brahe, was an ardent believer in astrology, and the brilliant young student and his equally brilliant teacher battled mightily over the effect of the rotations of the planets. Their arguments were so intense that they would wound each other with their words and retreat, not speaking for weeks at a time. Then they would make up and continue their work, until they would once again launch into the debate over the influence of the stars, renewing their rancorous fight.

Wishing to use the indisputable weight of scientific fact to bolster his evidence against his teacher, Kepler steeped himself in an exhaustingly detailed study of the stars. The study would make Kepler forever famous as an astronomer. But it also made Kepler a convert, forcing him to renounce his previous position. As his calculations and observations grew, the weight of the scientific evidence forced Kepler to become as profound a believer as his teacher in what he came to call "true astrology."

Among his many observations, Kepler noted a pattern to the astrologically important planetary angles—square, trine, conjunction, opposition, quadrature, sextile, etc.—as related to the total number of degrees in the circle. Expressing his discovery in fractions, the proportional relationship, he said, was $\frac{1}{2}$, $\frac{2}{3}$, $\frac{3}{4}$, $\frac{4}{5}$, $\frac{5}{6}$, $\frac{3}{5}$, and $\frac{5}{8}$. And, he found, if he straightened the circle into a violin string, the astrological angles corresponded to the divisions on which harmonics are based.

"The music God made during the Creation," he said, "He also taught nature to play; indeed, she repeats what He played to her."

Kepler further developed this theory into the concept of creationary resonance: the view that God creates humans with the gift of reading the mathematical harmonics of God's mind. Through this, he said, we can discover God's plan.

So, we must learn to dance.

That becomes increasingly important in the new era, for it is a time of harmony—and of living harmoniously—in all the meanings of the term. The Aquarian individual is noted for his or her individuality. But the Aquarian Age is also a time for individuals coming together, a time of unity. Although it may seem a contradiction, it is not. Because it is only when the individual has inner harmony, individual harmony, that he or she can live in harmony with others.

As we move deeper into the New Age, you will notice more acutely those who are moving out of step with the rhythm of the stars, for not all will pick up on that rhythm at once. For each, it will be a decision to participate, to join smoothly in the coming change or to resist. Some will be swept along, feeling lost in the changing world and the changing way of thinking. They may occasionally find themselves moving in time with it, moving smoothly with the flow; they may enjoy what they see happening around them, may personally benefit, even profit, finding themselves thanking their "lucky stars" when disaster seemed imminent and somehow they did not perish; but they will forever feel awkward and uncomfortable, stumbling when they most hoped to proceed. But for those who resist, there will be difficulty, problems in life, even pain and suffering.

To swim against the current is like fighting a rip current in the ocean that pulls you away from shore. As any good swimmer knows, to fight the current is to perish. To struggle against its pull is to flail uselessly until you tire yourself and sink below the surface to drown. If you flow with it, it will pull you swiftly some distance from the shore, then release you. Surviving a rip current depends on relaxing and letting it take you. So too with the spirit of the New Age.

The difference will be for those who choose to participate. For them, the transformation will be like gliding with the flow of cool water, peaceful and painless. To use the analogy of the sea again, think of how surfers learn to ride with the waves instead of just letting them crash over them haphazardly. So too with those who choose to ride with the current of the new era.

But there still will be the matter of learning to dance, constantly improving on it until it becomes effortless, just as a musician must first learn to read music and practice constantly at simple scales, then to play increasingly complicated arrangements until it seems—and is—effortless. As your skill and your abilities improve, the more pleasure you will get from it. The more you are in tune with it, the better you will feel.

It is not a matter of intellect. It is understanding. It comes from inside. Just as teaching yourself the names of the notes on a scale will not make you hear the music in your mind, analysis and reason will not by themselves bring understanding. They may help you see what is happening, but not *feel* it. You must go beyond that. You must gain insight, knowledge beyond the intellect. You must go past knowledge, to *knowing*.

In Siddha Yoga, mantra is the basis for knowing God. The scriptures of Shaivism say *mantra maheshwarah*, "Mantra is the supreme Lord." Swami Muktananda Paramahamsa, who brought Siddha Yoga to the world in *I Am That*, taught that the "basis of mantra is sound, and sound is the origin of the cosmos." *Spanda*, or vibration, is the primordial sound in which God originally manifested himself. It created the universe and continues to vibrate, pulsing continually through the universe and through ourselves. Repeating a mantra helps us get in tune with that vibration, in tune with ourselves, and in tune with the universe. It is learning to dance in rhythm with the stars.

But that does not necessarily mean you must sit and stare at a wall, chanting phrases or sounds that have no meaning for you. Mantras work for many. But you don't need the mantra. The power is not in it. The power is in you. The mantra may help you get in tune with the universe, may help you relax so that you can feel the spirit of the universe vibrating within you. But just as you do not have to be able to sing to listen to and appreciate music, you do not have to repeat a mantra incessantly to feel the vibration of the universe. Mantra is not the only way; it is *a tool.* The key to meditation is emptying the mind, becoming totally present in the moment, letting sensations and images flow into you and through you.

And that *is* the goal. The New Age is an age of effortless spirituality, of joining with God, the spirit of the universe, of finding the divinity within ourselves and around ourselves. In the words of the great mystic and poet William Blake:

*To see a world in a grain of sand*
*And a heaven in a wild flower,*
*Hold infinity in the palm of your hand*
*And eternity in an hour.*

—FROM *AUGURIES OF INNOCENCE*

Each of us is born with a divine spark that links us to the universe and to God.

To get in touch with that inner vibration, to touch the universal spark, you must let go of self-delusion and anger. You must open yourself to the possibilities—and live open to the apparently impossible. You must learn to look inside yourself. The path lies in reflection, in meditation. If you go to the river, to the sea, to the mountains, or stare at the clouds, you can meditate. It is not a question of where you are, but what you do. You can't think. You must truly meditate. Thinking is not meditation. When you think you are planning or remembering. Meditation is the zero-point, the essence. It is doing *nothing* and letting the moment happen all by itself. It is not thinking about the future, because the future is improbable, it hasn't happened yet. It is not thinking about the past; the past is already done; there is nothing you can do about it except try to apply the wisdom of the experience, the lesson you learned. Meditation is to stop thinking and just *be*. It's a stop in time, to have time to enjoy. If you hear something, if you smell something, if you touch something, it's beautiful.

To eat a fruit is meditation, if you let it be. If you let yourself feel the cool of an apple in your hand and against your lips before you bite into it; if you let yourself feel your teeth piercing the apple's skin, feel them sinking into the juicy flesh of the fruit, hear the sound of the crunch that comes with it; if you taste the apple's juice, feel it on your tongue as you chew; and if you let yourself follow that bite of apple as it flows down your throat when you swallow—that is meditation in action. That is letting yourself be totally in the moment, in the here and now. You are savoring the experience of eating that apple and you are savoring life.

If you think about them, the sounds and sensations, they become a science experiment instead of meditation. But if you just let them happen and, without thinking about them, let yourself marvel at the flood of feelings and sounds and tastes, then it is meditation.

Too many people go to the Louvre the way I used to—they look at a painting, then they're off to the next, and the next, and the next; rushing to get through it all so that they can see every piece of art. They're never stopping to enjoy the painting in front of them. They're thinking about how many more there are to see and how much time they have left to see them in. That's not the way the painters expected you to look at their work. It's not the way life expects to be seen, either. The artist put his or her soul into that one painting, to capture everything he or she was trying to say in that one piece of art. But it's not a telegram, it's a novel. It's an epic poem. It's something asking you to sit back and consider. It's something to savor. It is there for you to study the play of paint and shadow, to study the composition, the form—what was Mona Lisa really thinking with that wisp of an enigmatic smile playing on her lips?

If you do not take the time to savor that one painting for all the time it takes, you will have merely seen it. And as you rush from painting to painting at the museum, you will have seen the Louvre—but you will not *know* it, and you will not *understand.* Life is the same way. Meditation is the same way. It is the pause to savor, to relish this one moment, without worrying about the one just past or the one about to come. Life is meant to be savored. And when you can meditate in this one moment, when you can empty your mind and enjoy the nothingness, and the beauty, and the emptiness and the fullness, all at once—without thinking about it—then you will be able to savor life and savor every moment in it.

For you to absorb a piece of art or enjoy a piece of music—anything in life—it's not the end, it's a journey; enjoying the way, not anticipating the destination.

Men and women are accustomed to rushing to the end in everything they do. The goal is almost always more favored than the journey. And often upon arriving, we find it lacking. But if we take the time to look around, we can more greatly appreciate where we are when we arrive, because we better know where we have been.

Again, we can learn a lot from children. To them, the world is full of possibilities. They don't know what is impossible for them until they try. And for them, every event, every object, *everything*, is a source of absolute fascination. They come into the world completely open to everything, and they learn from everything. Watch them. They will study a blade of grass with the same fascination with which an adult will study a particularly engrossing film. They become lost in the blade of grass, feeling it, tasting it.

So many teachers of meditation say you have to put your hands just so, you have to sit just so. They try to make it a formula—a formula for achieving the perfect meditation. But the truly perfect meditation requires nothing more than your total presence in the present. It is emptiness that allows fullness. It is being totally aware. It is *being*.

The Zen masters compare it to emptying a cup. If a teacup is full, you can't put more in it, of course. When you try to pour in a new or different tea, it spills out of the cup, rather than into it. The same with your mind. If you are full of thoughts about tomorrow or yesterday, about what you think you should be doing or didn't get done, about what others may think, your mind is full and there is no place for the impressions of this moment. You are physically present in the here and now, but your mind "is miles away," as they say. Your spirit and your physical being are not in sync, and that makes it impossible for you to get in sync with the cosmic energy around you. That is why some choose mantras. Anything repetitive—chanting mantras, reciting a rosary—at first occupies the mind, blocking out thoughts distant from the moment, and finally numbs the mind, allowing it to relax and focus only on the instant at hand. But you can dance, whirling happily until you collapse from physical exhaustion, and find the same relaxation. Repeating mantras, then, is but a tool.

If it bothers you to do it, if you're uncomfortable in the position you're told to sit in, don't do it. That's not meditation. Meditation is not forced. It's just letting go. It is entering the stream of life and letting that stream carry you and flow through you. Meditation is the divine emptiness. It is the thunder of silence. By quieting yourself, quieting your mind, you open yourself to the concert playing around you.

You can meditate with music. Totally losing yourself in a fine piece of music—whatever that may be for you—is wonderful meditation. Entire audiences have broken into tears during the "Ode to Joy" in Beethoven's Symphony No. 9. They have become so rapt, so caught up in the rising power of the voices and the instruments, that the music carries them to a peak of emotion so high that it can only be released in a flood of joyous tears.

That is meditation in action. But how many people do you know who wander constantly with their stereo headphones on, blaring music so loud that you can hear it perfectly? If that works for meditation sometimes, that's wonderful. But constantly overpowering their senses with blaring music is more likely to be their cry of pain. They cannot find peace, so they try to block out the chaos around them. It does not lead to quiet if it is done all the time. It is like having someone beat a drum next to your head when you are trying to sleep. It is impossible to have peace without knowing how to find quiet.

That is the problem with too many chanters of mantras. They are not seeking to tune their internal instrument, using the mantra to guide them to get in tune with the vibration of the cosmos; they are blocking out the very sound they seek. How can you hear the song of a bird if you are constantly chanting "Om" or "hoo" or anything else? The bird is in perfect tune with the universe, but you will never know that because you are too busy trying to drown out its song with a phrase that holds no meaning for you.

Instead of chanting, you should listen with all of your being. The bird's song is the magic of the universe reaching out to you. It is one magical being reaching out to you, another magical being. The magic is in the air all around you and it is within you, in your own heart and mind. By letting yourself become a part of the energy flowing around you, you will charge your magical powers. But it is like the breeze. If you are rushing about, thinking of other things, you will never feel the gentle puff of wind touching your skin. You must be still, and quiet, and focused on this moment. Then you partake of what I call a "pause in eternity." There is no future; there is no past; there is only now.

Reaching that moment, you become one with the universe. You open yourself to the flow of energy, and you open yourself to the flood of knowledge, of wisdom, of *knowing* that flows with it. The Age of Aquarius is the age of truth and of true wisdom. True wisdom comes from your own personal knowledge. By opening yourself to every moment in its totality, you open yourself to experience everything—totally; you open yourself to know for yourself.

*Knowing* is very important in the New Millennium. This is the time for us to stop blindly believing what we are told. This is the time for us to go beyond beliefs. It is the time for us to challenge all that we have been taught to accept without question and build our beliefs for ourselves based on our own personal knowledge. We no longer will trust others to interpret holy words for us. We will look and learn and know for ourselves. By emptying ourselves and learning to be totally present in this moment, we will open ourselves to developing knowledge for ourselves. The more we become present and aware in every moment, the more we become aware of everything at every moment. And the more we become aware of everything, the more we will know for ourselves.

And when you are fully in this moment, just being without thinking, then you are free.

In that moment, when you are not self-conscious, thinking of how you might look to another, you are totally in tune with nature and totally natural. When you are not thinking, but just *being*, then you are not thinking about how your clothes fit, or how you look, or what another person is thinking. In that moment, you can let yourself *be*—with the universe, with yourself. And soon enough, the connection becomes obvious. You are not separate from the universe, you are not a visitor trying to see what it is really like, you are part of it. And just as it is divine, so are you. You are part of the perfect universe and you are perfect. In that way, putting meditation in action puts us at peace with ourselves. And that opens the way for us to be flooded with the peace that permeates this golden age.

As you can see, everything begins to interact and, in the end, the whole is greater than the sum of the parts. As we learn to *be*, we find peace and we begin to *know*; as we know more, we find more peace and learn to be even more in tune with the energy of the New Millennium.

When you let yourself carry that moment with you through every one of your moments, then you are totally free.

# 14

## Love in the New Age

Of all the changes that are sweeping around us as we move into the New Millennium, none is more fundamental and profound than the evolving changes in our concepts and forms of love.

We are entering the age of love, and in it the relationships between men and women, between men and other men, between women and other women—even between what we call "families"—will be altered dramatically and permanently. Every interaction between every one of us will be founded in pure love and friendship. The chains that bound us will be broken. The friendships and relationships based on convenience or personal benefit will come to an end. Now is the time for all of us to seek—and find—our spiritual twins, to unite with like souls or to reunite with those we have known in the past, so that we can move on to our combined future.

Now is the time for every one of us to find *true* love, total love, that is neither limited by traditions nor restricted by conventions.

This too will cause turmoil and difficulty before it is understood and accepted. Our changing concepts of love will shake our present relationships and our current institutions. We and our institutions will be forced to adapt to these changes or be destroyed by them. We no longer will rely on pieces of paper issued by the state or on seals of approval from religious leaders to sanctify and cement our unions. Unions outside of the law or outside of matrimony will not be considered immoral or sacrilegious, but unions without love will be.

It must be so in this coming age. Every great age of the Earth is affected by its opposing sign, by its polarity. Aries was touched by Libra. Where Aries emphasized the individual ego, the "me," Libra emphasized the unity of desires. Because of this, we saw the continuing wars of the age of Aries, when people sought to impose their wills and their egos over others; but we also saw the great cultural developments of the Greeks, the Libran balance and grace that showed itself in their art and architecture. The powerful determination of Taurus brought with it the sense of "I desire" and the solid pyramids that still stand as symbols of permanence and human aspiration. But its complement, Scorpio, influenced tremendously with its spirit of domination, its sense of "I possess." Now comes the Age of Aquarius, of unity and humanity. But that energy is multiplied in the New Millennium because the positive aspect of Aquarius is magnified by its polarity. The opposite sign of Aquarius is Leo, the heart—love.

That is why this is called the era of love, peace, and union. In it, we will find ourselves able to give and receive unconditional love. We will abandon the love that expresses itself as "I love you if ... " There will be no conditions, no demands. Love will be given and received because it is felt, not because it is needed or because we want something in return.

It may be hard to conceive of this fabled love becoming reality. Love itself is a word that has been used so badly that it is tryingly difficult to remember and understand what it really means.

To many, love is only a way to dominate another person. They seem to be saying, "I'll keep loving you if you do this for me." For those, love is only a way to control others, to get them to do things, or to give things. But that is not love, that is emotional prostitution. Users of these tactics are trading their so-called love in exchange for something, either material things or services. Their expression of love is but a coin used to purchase those things or services.

The other side of that coin is the person who accepts it as payment. People like that are the ones who want so desperately to be loved that they try to buy it with gifts and actions. There is nothing wrong, in fact just the opposite, with giving someone you care about a present. But there is something definitely wrong when you give the present only as a way to get someone to say, "I love you."

True love does not require gifts or services or even words. True love, which comes from the joining of complementary souls and the sharing of mutual energy, is known without the need for expression. True love is just that: it is true, and truth need not be spoken.

Too many of us say "I love you" just to get another person to say it to us. We say it so we can hear it. We say it without really meaning it because somehow we think that when we hear it in return it is true. We have not learned to love ourselves so we want someone to do it for us.

But we all know when someone really loves us without having to hear it. A mother who feels love for her child does not have to speak of that love to her child. She shows it in the way she strokes that child's hair once her infant has gone to sleep. She shows it by sitting up through the night and hugging her child tightly when that child is sweating with fever and crying in discomfort. Not a word of love is spoken, but a lullaby or the calming coos of the mother say more than a million "I love you's" could ever accomplish.

Similarly, we know that we are loved for real when we turn and find our partner simply smiling with that special glow in his or her eyes that tells us exactly how he or she feels. We know that we love when we find ourselves looking over someone we care about as he or she sleeps, a smile on our lips, without that person even knowing that we are looking. And sometimes, to show the power of our thoughts, we can see the same satisfied smile paint itself across that sleeping person's lips as we watch.

There is nothing wrong with saying "I love you" when you mean it. Of course not. Our feelings often form thoughts that spill out into words before we even realize we are speaking. But there is a huge difference between simple expressions of our sentiments because they are what we are feeling and trying to build feelings by repeating the words over and over.

Love in the New Millennium is a love that is experienced. It has no demands. It needs no expression or words. It is felt with the very soul because it comes from the very soul. In feeling it, it is recognized and felt by others. It is a love that encompasses much more. And it is not limited to only one person. True love—love in the New Millennium—is much more open. It is not exclusive. You can love your spouse and love your career and love God and love your friends. That idea of "you belong to me" is dead. So too will the idea that because "you suffer for me, then you must love me" will be dead. Love does not hurt, it enriches.

When complementary spirits come together, it is the union of yin and yang. It multiplies the energy of each giver-recipient. Giving love does not deplete our reservoir of energy, it expands it. Giving love gives us strength. Giving love without demands, without conditions, brings us not just in union with another soul, but closer to union with the universal spirit. Giving love helps connect us to that vast reservoir of energy that is the cosmic consciousness, the essence of existence, the well of all power and knowledge.

Giving allows us to receive and as we let the spirit of the new era flow into us, we will find ourselves more and more willing and able to surrender to love without fearing it. We will not need to have our love certified by a signed document that obligates us to each other. We will not need to exchange vows. Love in the Age of Aquarius is a love without limits. It is a love without barriers. It is a love that goes beyond the flesh, beyond physical concepts of beauty and of ugliness, beyond age—beyond everything.

In the New Millennium we will learn that true love simply *is*. It exists on its own. It is a reality. It doesn't have to be examined, questioned, proven, or tested. It doesn't bind or limit, it frees. If I love you and you are with me, that is wonderful; if not, I can still love you and you can go about your business and that is just fine. Love is not measured or weakened by distance, either. If we love each other we will love each other just as intensely whether we are touching or whether we are oceans apart. There will be no need or place for jealousy. We will love each other, still, no matter who else we happen to be with at the moment.

This changing form of thinking will not open the doors to an era of so-called free love in which we jump from partner to partner experimenting with sex. Instead, we will seek—and find—spiritual love. Sex will become what it is: just one form of physical expression of that spiritual love. And we will lose our sense of guilt associated with love and sex.

In the 1960s, hippies spoke of the Age of Aquarius and free love. Everyone was supposed to feel free to love everyone else without restriction or limitation. But the word "love" in that use quickly came to mean merely sex. Love lost its spiritual meaning; even its physical meaning was reduced to being simply a synonym for the procreative act, rather than as an expression of a deeper and more spiritual sentiment.

In many ways, the free love movement of the world's youth at that time was but a way of rebelling against the ways of their parents. Throughout the Age of Pisces, love and sex became inseparable. There could be in that form of thinking but one love partner and one sexual partner. Yet often enough, the children of the sixties saw their parents locked in loveless marriages. Many of those marriages were not even born of love in the first place. They could just as easily be brought about out of convenience or what was considered sensible. Rich families encouraged their rich children to marry each other, a modern variation of the antiquated concept of joining kingdoms through marriage.

Even when those marriages were based in love, they frequently were not based in equality. The institution of marriage perpetuated the dominance of males, with the full backing of church dictates and governmental laws. Even our societal norms relegated women to the house as men went out to conquer in the world of business.

Now, in the Age of Aquarius, men and women themselves are changing. Women are finally stepping out from the dominating shadow of men, shedding their subservient roles of the past and insisting on their rightful place in the order of the universe as equals. Obviously, this has been a long time coming. Women have been fighting for—and winning—their rights for decades, but now they are tackling the last vestiges of patriarchal domination. Their victories are victories for both genders, whether they are recognized as such or not.

In the natural order of the universe, energy flows with both masculine and feminine force, in combination. Yin and yang, Mother Earth and Father Sky, are all equal and equally deserving of our respect. None is more powerful than the other. They are complementary forces that act in unison to bring balance to the universe.

In early agricultural societies, people venerated both the feminine and the masculine aspects equally, allotting the growing and harvest seasons to the feminine mother and the cold winters when the ground lay dormant to the power of the father. But under the patriarchal influence of Pisces, the feminine forces fell into disfavor, subjugated by images of a male god. Under Christianity, Eve's birth from Adam's rib set the stage for women always to come second behind men, in God's eyes and in men's; her seduction in the Garden of Eden added the permanent guilt of responsibility for the Original Sin to the load women were expected to bear, relegating them for all time hence to a position of inferiority. Men took their masculine roles, wearing blue instead of pink and never letting themselves be seen crying. Women stayed home to care for the children.

Now comes the time of integration between the masculine and feminine once again. The unifying energy of Aquarius puts an end to the dichotomy of the past. There will be no more differences, no more differentiation, no more opposites. Now, not only do women want to be seen as equal to men, but men want to recapture that aspect of their nature. Once again comes the blending of the spiritual energies within us and the integration of both aspects of the divinity inside each of us, for the benefit of all humanity.

As we ourselves change, it is only natural that our relationships change as well.

All of our relationships in the Age of Pisces were tainted by the negative spirit of the age. Relationships between men and women were no different. Too often, marriages became caricatures of what they were meant to be. They practically followed a scripted course, with men and women playing roles in a play.

Think about it. In the beginning, the woman was the perfect, immaculate virgin; the man was equally perfect, and masculine. Everything was perfect in the first few months. They called each other "my dear" and "my love." Then, as time went on, the masks began to crack and fall away. It was no longer necessary to put on an act to attract someone; they were already trapped. The man started to walk around in his underwear, the woman in a robe with no makeup on. The brilliance of that first enchantment started to fade as the reality showed through, and they entered the phase of compromises. They said, "You're like this and I'm like this, but let's try to get along." "I know he snores, but I can sleep in another room or get him to roll over if it bothers me too much."

Then came what is known as the seven-year itch, when the man and woman said to themselves that they'd had enough. They were fed up. Sex had been reduced to a boring, repetitive act among couples who were afraid or incapable of experimenting and discovering. At one time, submissive women even had to put up with verbal and physical abuse. The itch sent both husbands and wives seeking gratification outside of their marriages, clandestinely. They had flings or affairs with others. Yet the duality of the Piscean Age, the ongoing conflict between the spirit and the flesh, caused most to maintain a facade of harmony at home. Couples who fell victim to this malaise did not seek to repair their union nor to dissolve it. They merely lived comfortable, or uncomfortable, lies that— as with all lies—sparked internal discord and feelings of guilt within the "cheating" party or eventually crumbled and were exposed.

Seeing this, the youth of the sixties aimed part of their rebellion at love itself and settled for a sexual revolution. They wound up breaking down Victorian barriers and shattering Piscean precepts, but the victory was hollow. In a way, the devastating plague of AIDS that still afflicts us is the direct outcome of the misguided revolution of the sixties. Since the concept of free love became a shallow cliché for promiscuity, the cosmic pendulum of cause and effect eventually swung back to force us to reflect on what the proponents of the movement had achieved: a sex-related disease of the flesh that was, in karmic terms, the manifestation of a sex-related disease of the spirit. In other words, having ignored the spirituality of love in exchange for the physical pleasure of sex, we saw a physical disease come upon us to make us slow down and consider our spirituality.

This is in no way to be taken to mean that AIDS sufferers are being punished or that they are being "damned" for their past actions. That is a Piscean concept of invoking shame or fear rather than understanding. But the fact remains that the disease itself has forced us to be more thoughtful about our physical expressions of our sexual urges and to consider more the spiritual expression of our love.

Now comes the time to discard our old ideas of sex and love. Sex in and of itself is not love. It can be a way of expressing love; but one is not dependent on the other. The sharing of feelings in physical terms is one way to show we care. But it can also be a simple sharing of physical pleasure. We can love someone without having sex with them. We can have sex with someone without loving them. Sex and love should not be bound together as restrictions upon, or definitions of, one another. Neither needs to be restricted by feelings of guilt or of obligation. You should not be required to have sex with someone just because you love them. But neither should sex be a boundary, a dividing line between concepts of purity and impurity. Sex is purely physical; love—in its truest form—is purely spiritual.

Now our awakening spirituality takes us beyond thinking of love in terms of a purely physical act and beyond thinking that we can love only one other. In the New Millennium, we will seek love with our souls and find love taking us to join in new unions of similar souls. Often enough, they will be souls we have known before.

You may already find yourself meeting people whom you feel you have known before, people you feel immediate kinship with. Or you may find yourself seeking people of this sort, feeling unfulfilled in your relationships and your friendships. This is the spirit of the New Age flowing through you, sending you in search of the soul mates you need to link with once again so that you may pass through this time of transition. This is the time for us to come together in spiritual families that go beyond mere unions of blood and flesh.

We are all born into one family, born of a single union of a man and a woman. And there is a reason: the family we are born into is our karmic family. In this, our first family on this plane, we come to learn or help deliver a lesson. Because we return to this plane only to continue learning, our first family may be made up of those who we have wronged in the past, or it may be made up of those we helped in the past. If, for example, we had difficulty controlling our anger at one time and lashed out at our children, we may return this time to be a child—and our parents in this life may have been our children before—so that we may all learn to forgive and to love without anger. Or we may return as a parent to the same child again, so that we may all try this time to live in love without anger.

At one time, you may have been rich, with little or no compassion for the less fortunate. This time, you may return to a poor family that is rich in love, so that you may learn the value of love and the reason for compassion. Or you may have been poor once before, and you return to a family of relative wealth, so that you can demonstrate for them the value of what you learned in that previous life.

The cycle of incarnations exists only for lessons. Once they are learned, the cycles end and we can go on to join permanently with the universal spirit. The family we are born into exists to help us with that lesson. But that does not mean that we are always born into the same family, cycle after cycle. It may be that you have come into a family that exists to help prepare you for later lessons in life, to ready you for meetings with other souls that you have known before. The lesson for the souls who are the parents this time around may be to learn to care for another. The lesson for you may be how to learn from that and use that knowledge in your own union with another later in life. The intolerant must learn tolerance; the selfish must learn sharing; and so on.

But whether you are born into a family of souls you have known before or not, you will find yourself meeting with souls you have known as you go on through your life. And in the New Millennium, you will not just meet them, you will join with them. With each passing day, you will be more atune, more able to recognize those souls, and more able to recognize why you are supposed to join with them.

In this way, you will find yourself forming spiritual unions with others, forming the spiritual families that will form the basis of our relationships in the new era. As you open yourself more to the spirit of the New Age, you also will find yourself recognizing kindred spirits and joining with them. Those points of light that are now shining here and there will find themselves coming together to illuminate the way for others.

That is the meaning and the purpose of spiritual families. We come together not because of physical attraction or need, but because of mutual feelings and thoughts. Our unions then become like a magnet that draws us to others and draws others to us. In this way, the Aquarian spirit of unity and spirituality grows to encompass all.

Jesus Christ himself condemned the concept of the supremacy of biological families, of bloodlines being stronger than spiritual ties. Even though his words have been used for two thousand years in defense of the sanctity of the family, he

was in fact a forceful and revolutionary opponent of the traditional family and an advocate of unions of like souls in spiritual families.

The Book of Mark, Chapter 3, tells of how Jesus was preach-
ing in the synagogue and was told that his brethren and his
mother were outside and wanted to see him. His answer began
with a question: "Who is my mother, or my brethren? ...
whosoever shall do the will of God, the same is my brother, and
my sister, and mother."

As he was dying on the cross, Christ again repeated this same
theme when Mary came to see him. Christ told one of his disciples to take her as a new mother and Mary to take the disciple as her son. Christ was telling them both to see each other as
part of the same spiritual family, that Mary was the mother of
all men, and the disciple should see in every mother his own.

Now, as we make Christ's message of loving our neighbors a
reality, we also make a reality of his advocacy of unions of
grander, spiritual families. In this new way of thinking, we will
identify all of the kindred spirits that we encounter as our
brethren. The friend that you make along the way will become
as much a brother or sister, or daughter or son, as one of blood;
and you will recognize them as such. You will open your house
to them. And they will open theirs to you. Those kindred spirits will seek kindred spirits to be with, and they will draw them
to you as well. Their spouses, then, will become as much a part
of your family as they are. And the children they bear together
will be as much yours as theirs.

Soon enough, this network of unions will grow into communities—communes, of a sort—in which all share mutual
concerns and all share mutually. Just as you would not deny
food to a member of your own family, you will not deny food
to the members of your spiritual family. Just as all within a fam-

ily are expected to do their part for the family, so too will all within the spiritual family be expected to contribute their part to the betterment of all in it.

I know this sounds alarmingly like the failed communes of the sixties, or worse, like communism—far from it! Communism, like all isms, involved an imposition of will upon others. It involved domination. It involved control. And it became a trap. Born into it, you could not choose to leave it. The communes of the sixties were based on the rejection of almost everything modern society had to offer—both the good and the bad. It often meant living in shacks built from scraps, living "off the land," and rejecting all forms of technology. They became, in their way, just as much an imposition of will as that which those in them were seeking to leave behind.

But in families, we are equally pleased when one of our children chooses to be an attorney and another chooses to be a farmer. We are equally pleased when one finds pleasure or even a vocation with a computer, and another with an artist's paintbrush. We don't—or at least shouldn't—force anyone in our family to reject worldly goods, nor to dedicate themselves to acquiring them. Instead, we do—or should, anyway—share a love that unites us regardless of the particulars of our individual lives.

So too with spiritual families. They are not trade unions nor religious orders. Spiritual families are ever-growing unions of like souls brought together by love—where we are all brethren and every child is everyone's child. We may choose to live together in one house. We may choose to build our houses together into communities. Or just as it happens in biological families, we may maintain our union across continents, with some of us living in one place and others living in another. Certainly, our affinity for each other's company will make us want to share our time together. But the link of love among us will remain as strong no matter where we choose to live or how near or far we are from one another.

This is a whole new concept of love and of family, I know. But in the spirit of the New Age, we will not be forced to forsake our individuality for the unity of the group, nor will we have to forsake unity in order to retain our independence. What we will achieve is shared freedom, based in love.

# 15

# The Seven Keys

No matter who you are, no matter where you come from, no matter what path you choose to arrive at the way of Aquarius, you must learn the seven keys to living in the New Millennium. They are the keys to developing the new person, the person who can seize hold of the true meaning of the new era and realize the fullness of his or her humanity. They are the principles to guide us in every moment of the New Millennium, and they are as interrelated to each other as we all are interrelated with each other in the cosmic tapestry of the universal spirit. To make the seven keys the guiding principles of your life is to open yourself to the full potential of the New Millennium and to realize your own full potential in it so that you can transmit that energy back into the universe and add to the growing power of the New Age.

The keys are simple and simply stated; but to make them true guiding principles of your being is somewhat like understanding the real meaning of a Zen koan—logic may help you understand the intellectual meaning, but truly "getting it" comes from somewhere beyond logic. Where does my fist go when I open my hand? What is the sound of one hand clapping? There are logical explanations that can yield intellectually satisfying, or at least intellectually sufficient, answers. But the *true* answer cannot be explained. You either get it or you don't. It is similar to what George Bernard Shaw once said of explaining a joke: It's like dissecting a frog, he said—you'll understand how they work, but they both die in the process.

It's the same with the seven keys to living in the New Millennium. You can know them and you can understand them intellectually, but until they become a part of you that exists without thinking about them, without forcing yourself, you haven't really "got" them. You should, and must, practice them every day. Then one day you will realize that you are no longer thinking about them, you are living them. But you must practice. In that way, learning to make the seven keys a part of your life is like learning to swim. At first, you spend your time thinking about holding your breath, about how to place your hands and arms in the water, about how to kick. It is awkward and, often, frustrating. Then, for some quickly and for others more slowly, the motions begin to fall together. You stop thinking about your breathing and concentrate on placing your hands at precisely the right angle for maximum thrust. And then one day you realize that you are no longer thinking about the act of swimming at all; you find yourself instead thinking about where you are swimming to or from or merely about the sheer joy of gliding through the water.

So too with the guiding principles that are already becoming a part of your life. Every day, when you get up in the morning, you should look at them and make the simple affirmation that today you are going to live by them. Every night, before you go to sleep, you should review them and remind yourself of where and how you succeeded. That's all there is to it. But, like learning what truly is the sound of one hand clapping, it is a difficult process with a simple solution.

Here, then, are the seven keys:

1. Valor
2. Love
3. Truth
4. Meditation
5. Awe
6. Daring
7. Virtue

First, the guiding principle that will open the way for all the rest: valor. With valor, courage, bravery, we will be able to let go of the fear that has gripped us throughout the era of Pisces. By letting go of fear, we will be able to open ourselves to the new lessons that await us. If we cling to our fear, we will not allow ourselves to question; if we do not question, we cannot learn. This is fundamental. The new era will be built by those who don't just accept the facts handed to them, who do not rely solely on faith, but build their faith on the solid foundation of personal knowledge. What we know for ourselves to be true cannot be questioned.

Think of the sky. We *know* the sky is blue, not just because someone told us it is blue, but because we can see it for ourselves. If someone told us that the sky is red, we would know that that is not true. The truths we seek in the new era also must come from personal knowledge, so that we will not blindly follow the teachings of any group or person. The Age of Aquarius is the era of light. There can be no blindness. It is the time for all of us to see for ourselves. Armed with this new knowledge, we will come to understand for ourselves the true meaning of the teachings of the Bible, the Bhagavad Gita, the Koran. We will not need others to interpret them for us. We will know the principles of the Ten Commandments from within our hearts. We will know the true difference between right and wrong, and what is right and wrong, without needing someone else to tell us. We will not need someone to tell us the law, we will know the proper law from within our very selves.

This is a frightening thought for many people. It is a frightening thought for institutions that get their strength from our doubts and fears. Try to imagine a world without courts or judges and you can see why the very thought of losing these institutions is frightening. We expect someone else to tell us what to do, how to behave. We also expect them to tell everyone around us how to behave, because that is the only way we know how to interact. But in the Age of Aquarius, we will each know what is right and wrong for ourselves. Our personal and societal rules will be the same. This does not happen overnight. We cannot, should not, discard our institutions or our laws yet. Anarchy is not the answer. But as we all come in step and in tune with the spirit of the times, as we all find our own spirituality, then we will find these written laws and rules superfluous. And the courts and the judges will fade away from disuse as they are necessary only when people disagree. Once we all abide by the same rules, the rules that come from within us—rules that hold humanity in supreme regard, rules that are by their nature humanitarian—we will not have the discord that makes the courts necessary. Aquarius is the sign of harmony; disharmony is what makes the courts, laws, and judges necessary.

But it will take true valor, individual and collective courage, to step beyond the safe realm of known society to forge the society of tomorrow. Stepping into the unknown world of the future, with no guideposts to direct us, requires reaching into our inner wells of knowledge to find the strength that comes from knowing that what we are doing is, in every way, correct.

There will be those people and groups, as you know, who will resist the teachings of the New Age for as long as they can. And there will be many who, lost in their personal doubt and fear, will look to a self-appointed leader, not accepting that the only path to follow is the one that our own hearts and minds dictate.

But the path to discovery is found by looking within, not by looking without, no matter how alluring the appeal. Only then, once we have journeyed deep into ourselves, can we look outside with the new knowledge we have gained and see each other as we really are, accepting our differences and our flaws. It takes courage, it takes valor, to challenge the teachings of a lifetime, especially when these teachings have been handed down from generation to generation and are defended by powerful institutions like churches and temples.

But look at the cruelties in the name of faith and beware. Native Americans were burned at the stake to force them to adopt the God of the missionaries. Non-Catholics were tortured by the tribunals of the Inquisition. As Pisces peaked at its heavenly zenith, the horrors of the so-called good over the imagined evil of the time peaked as well.

Now is the time for true good to prevail. The Age of Aquarius will lead us to consider the good in terms of all humanity. But this is not just a matter for the mind, a matter of intellect; good comes from the heart, which must be guided by the second principle of the New Millennium: love.

The second principle, love, is so important that I devoted the whole of the past chapter to it and to how love will change in the New Millennium. But as a principle, this key means love in the physical sense and love in the spiritual sense; love for ourselves and love for others. Once again, the path to discovery begins with an inward journey. If we truly love ourselves, we can truly love others. If we have not learned to love ourselves, then we take our partners out of need. We seek someone to fulfill us, instead of fulfilling ourselves and finding someone we want to share ourselves and our time here with.

When we love ourselves in all of its meanings, love our flaws and our foibles, then we can see the true beauty that shines within each of us. To look outside at physical definitions of beauty, at standards of beauty imposed by advertising and upbringing, is to look at only the superficial aspect of ourselves rather than at the totality of ourselves. In the Age of Aquarius, we will find true love first within ourselves, then look outside to see the beauty of those around us.

Love brings compassion. No one is perfect, not now and not in the New Millennium. But just as love of ourselves allows us to accept our own flaws, true love allows us to accept others for what they are, with all of their flaws, as well. We love our children even when they throw a tantrum and we get angry at them. We can love others in the same way. We may not accept or be pleased with everything they do, but we won't love them less. And our mutual love will make us all try a little harder not to annoy or trouble others because we will care enough about them to not want to see them disturbed.

Third, and fundamentally linked to the other principles, is the principle of truth, both the goal and the basis for all the others in the New Age. We seek and will discover true love. We seek and will discover true valor. With these, we will prepare ourselves to discover truth. Truth also comes from within rather than from without. It is founded in personal knowledge. And rather than separating us, it will join us, because truth is undeniable. There is no "your truth" and "my truth." There is only the truth. As we each look inside ourselves to find this truth, we will find ourselves discovering the things that we all know to be true.

Did you really need someone to tell you it is wrong to kill? No, of course not. Other truths are not as obvious, but just as fundamental. As we look deep inside ourselves, we find that "do unto others" is more than just a saying; it really is what we all wish for and deserve. In the New Age, we will be free to live this way, because we will each find the truths that we share in common. These are universal truths. In some cases, these will be all new truths. Things that we can't imagine today we will know to be true in the world of tomorrow. But then if someone had told the Pilgrims that someday we would fly in a matter of hours across the ocean it took them weeks to cross, they would think we were lying or crazy. If someone had told Mozart that someday astronauts would listen to his music as they stepped onto the Moon, Mozart might have stopped writing music as he pondered whether the lunacy was ours or his. But now we know both flight and lunar landings not only to be true, but commonplace. Some of the truths of the new era will be the same. Incredible though they may seem from the perspective of what we have known in the long Age of Pisces, they will be self-evident in the New Millennium, the Age of Aquarius.

You may have already glimpsed some of these truths, then shaken yourself and called them impossible. But in the new era ahead, we can make the impossible possible if we think it can be and believe it enough. That has been true in any age, but even more so now.

Great thinkers of long ago have seen things that only now are coming true. Think of da Vinci or Jules Verne. Da Vinci drew a blueprint for a helicopter, a device that would not fly until five hundred years after his death. Verne envisioned us traveling beneath the oceans of the Earth and traveling to the face of the Moon in a rocket ship, and his writings were called science fiction. Now, of course, we think nothing of having a rocket lifting off every week taking satellites to circle the globe or taking men to travel in an orbiting laboratory for months at a time.

It is no accident that these things only now are coming to fruition. The Age of Aquarius is the age of technology and space exploration.

But there will be many who will resist the truth of the new era. They may try at first by playing upon the sense of self-doubt that lies within each of us. Self-doubt exists only because we have allowed others to define our reality for so long that we no longer know what is real anymore. When we look inside and catch the first sight of what *is* real and it does not concur with what those around us have said and are saying at the moment, we discard it. We doubt ourselves because we have allowed others to tell us what truth is. But as we reach deeper into the New Age, we will reach deeper inside ourselves for the truth. And as we learn the truth, we will no longer need or want others to interpret it for us. This will cause friction with those who defend the institutions they feel comfortable with, the institutions that they cling to like a security blanket in a world they really aren't very comfortable with at all. Those who cannot, or do not dare, to look inside themselves for the truth will be the ones who will resist the rest of us the most. They will be the ones who challenge the rest of us the most. They will be the ones who try to make the rest of us think that we are wrong because they want desperately to believe that they are right, and they know that once their faith is shaken, they have nothing left to cling to. But be wary of anyone who demands that you have blind faith in what they are saying. If they will not allow scrutiny, it is probably because their beliefs cannot stand up to scrutiny. And when those who hide within the institutions because they do not dare to look inside themselves feel that they are losing their grip on the rest of us, they will fight.

In the New Age, also, we will no longer fall prey to guilt. Truth will set us free. Guilt is a concept built on fear, on letting others decide our truths for us. It has power over us only if we let others have power over us. Guilt is an admission that others are setting the rules of our behavior. But they are also an admission that we have not yet accepted ourselves as our own guides.

They are an admission that we cannot decide for ourselves what is right and what is wrong, that we are only trying to avoid doing what someone else has decided is wrong. Once we realize the truth for ourselves, we will lose our doubt, and no one can make us feel guilty.

This does not mean that we can pretend that we know the truth when we really do not and use this as an excuse for our behavior. Knowing the truth will not permit us to act in a way that is offensive to others. Knowing the truth brings us in tune with the cosmic truth. As more and more people become attuned, we will notice that our behaviors coincide without us needing to impose rules of behavior on anyone. None of us can lead others to the truth; they must find it for themselves. If we find ourselves trying to make others fit our mold, then we have not yet found the truth. That is the same as being forced by others to fit into their predescribed molds, which is exactly what we will find ourselves rebelling against.

In the New Age, each must follow the path dictated by his or her own heart. We will *know* what is right and, knowing this, we will not permit others to try to draw us into their conception of right and wrong. Knowing it for ourselves, we will only feel sorry for those who have not yet seen the light; we will feel sorry for those who have not yet found the truth that the rest of us know.

The fourth key to living in the New Millennium helps us find truth and love and valor and all of the other keys we need. The fourth key is meditation.

Every moment of every day, we must be totally, fully, completely aware of that one moment. To do that, we must put meditation into action; we must put ourselves in that tranquil state of hyperrealization that allows us to truly feel and experience what is happening at that moment. We must be totally and absolutely present in the here and now so that we can savor every wonder of the universe. This is how we recognize not only the splendor and magnificence of everything around us, but also recognize our connection to it all.

A sunset is beautiful, bathing everything in an orange and golden glow of light and warmth. It washes over and through us and everything around us, a light from the heavens reaching across the vastness of space to shower us with the very essence of life. From that light comes the basic stuff that fuels the plants that feed the animals—and through the plants and the animals to feed us. Standing in its midst, that light of life flows around you and through you. It becomes a part of you, and you a part of it. That moment at sunset is more than symbolic—it is an absolute testament to our interconnectedness with everything and everyone around us; to your place in and as part of the entire universe. Meditating upon it, you not only open yourself to recognize the vastness of the eternal link between the essence of the universe and all that lies within it, but you help to strengthen it. Your meditation not only opens your perceptions and the powers of your mind to new and unplumbed reaches, but connects you to the absolute and unlimited power of the universal *one*.

Putting meditation into action, in every moment, allows you to recognize that everything is sacred within the universe. The ground you step on is sacred. The leaves on the trees are sacred. You are sacred. Everything is sacred and everything is divine, because everything is connected to the almighty essence of being.

To live fully in every moment, to live every moment to the fullest through meditation, is to open yourself to find the wonder of the universe and to open yourself to the fifth key to living in the New Millennium: awe.

To live in awe is to allow yourself to marvel at all that the universe offers, from the grand to the minuscule. There is as much to be awed by in the work of an ant as there is in the wonder of the Grand Canyon. Both are the incredible work of the universal spirit through the eons; both are the perfect developments of the cosmic design.

Just as there is a reason that every event happens, there is a reason that everything is exactly as it is, when it is. This alone should be awe inspiring—to know that all the forces of the universe have worked together to lay out this grand stage for you to be a part of. This perfect plan has opened a place for you to be both actor and audience, to be both participant and spectator.

But to live in awe is not just to be awestruck by the beauty and wonder of the universe, not just to be astonished by how infinitely complex yet simple it all is, but to respect that marvelous interconnection and interrelatedness of everything within the universe, including you.

To live in awe is to recognize the divinity that flows through every tiny particle of the universe, including yourself, and to recognize the infinite wonder of the universal divinity that is its source—and to be inspired by it. You are an integral part of the whole, of the one, and every one of your actions and thoughts impacts the whole, sending out ripples throughout the entirety of the cosmos like a stone dropped into a pond. Likewise, every ripple in the larger pond affects you.

But living in awe is not just to stand in slack-jawed wonder at the vastness of the whole, but to allow yourself to marvel at its most minute component, at every instant in its infinity of being. That is why living in awe and putting meditation into action are so closely linked as keys to living in the New Millennium.

As I told you before, if you do not allow yourself to live in the moment, if you are always looking to the future, you end up living like a horse with blinders on—always looking ahead to something that is coming, and never recognizing that which is all around you. Letting yourself live in awe of the moment opens you to marvel at the changing current of energy as it flows in around you, and allows you to become a part of it.

This is not a race. The more you are open to join in the flow of spirit sweeping in with the New Age, the sooner you will be able to recognize yourself flowing with it. In this way, the ever-increasing influence of the New Millennium not only flows into you, but you flow into it. You lend your strength to bringing about the change even as you draw strength from it. You receive calming and invigorating energy from the universal spirit, and you transmit your own calming and invigorating energy into it. Living in awe, as I use the term, allows you then to not just watch as the world changes, not just to witness the play of life as it unfolds, but to recognize your active role in life and in eternity. Your thoughts, your feelings, your actions, are as powerful an influence in the New Millennium as the influence of the New Age is on you.

Which brings us to the sixth key to living in the New Millennium: daring.

The Age of Aquarius is the age of light, the age of illumination, the age of wisdom, and the age of love. But you must dare to let all of these things into your life so that you can take part of the new life that lies ahead. This takes courage. It also takes daring.

To fully participate in all that the New Millennium has to offer, you must take chances—you must experiment with life. Life is an adventure and if you are not adventurous, if you are not daring, then you will not savor all that life has to offer. We each can choose to stay locked inside our homes and locked inside ourselves. This way, we rationalize, we protect ourselves from the dangers that lurk outside. Locked inside ourselves, we shield ourselves from the possible pain of lost love. If we let no one in, we risk no danger of falling in love and having our relationship fail.

But as the poet said: better to have loved and lost than never to have loved at all. By locking ourselves in, by avoiding the risks, we miss the adventure of life. We step out of the play and into the audience. It is the difference between watching others eat and taking a huge bite for yourself. No matter how well that other diner describes the experience, no matter what pleasure or displeasure we take in watching him eat, it will never be the same as tasting the feast for yourself.

And life is a feast laid out for us all to partake of. It is for our pleasure and for our wisdom. If you never take risks, if you never allow yourself to experiment with life, then you can never know its fullness. If you shield yourself to protect yourself from disappointment and despair, you also shield yourself from excitement and ecstasy. The very reason that we ride roller coasters is because we want the thrill of the ups and downs and twists and turns; no matter how long you stand and watch others on a roller coaster, it will never compare to riding it yourself.

If you do not experiment, you will not experience. That is why you must be daring. That doesn't mean we all have to go out and take up bungee jumping or lion taming tomorrow. It means daring to let your emotions show, daring to let people into your heart, daring to dive into the deep end of a cold pool and letting the shock of the water's chill hit you with all its force. It means opening your mind and letting its power take you beyond where you are, into the unknown. That is how you truly open yourself to the wonder of life and to the wonder of the universe.

Daring to live means letting go of your fears. If you love someone and that loved one leaves, so be it. Think of all you will have missed if you never let that person in—the intimacy, the chance to hold hands and walk barefoot in the damp sand of the shoreline, the chance to laugh deeply over something shared.

Daring to live means opening yourself to opportunities. If you don't dare to go to the party, you will never meet the person of your dreams. They may not be at the party, but they certainly aren't going to suddenly materialize in the rut that you walk in between your television set and your refrigerator.

And daring in the New Millennium means daring to be yourself. It means being bold enough to shed the facades, the masks, the devices, and let others see the real you. It means daring to be natural. Let others see the joy you get from the simplest things—from the flight of a bird or the shape of a cloud, from the phrases of a piece of music or the movement of your own body. It takes daring to drop the devices of a lifetime that we have learned to use to shield our inner selves from the outside, to drop the layers of protective behaviors we have developed like the calluses of a workman's hand, to peel away the masks we wear to act out the part we have prepared for ourselves in life, and let others see not the actor in the play, but the person you really are.

Not everyone will like what they see when you dare to be yourself. So be it. There will be many, many more who will love what they see. There will be many who will be drawn to your ingenuity, to your honesty, to your daring itself.

The seventh, and final, guiding principle of the New Millennium is virtue, the golden principle of the new era, the key that brings together all the other keys in harmony.

To live in virtue means to live in honesty, with respectfulness, with compassion, and with tolerance. The New Millennium, as you well know, is the era of unity and individuality. So to fully partake in the way of the dawning age, you must let your individuality show honestly and you must be honest in everything you do and say.

Honesty begins with being honest with yourself. You can read this book a hundred times, a thousand times, but if you do not honestly open yourself to the principles in it, it will remain merely a collection of words and pages. If you seek love for love's sake, to fill a need in yourself instead of honestly opening yourself to it by beginning with love for yourself, then you will never find true love. Honesty is the starting place for all virtue, opening the way for you to know yourself, to know others, and to know the all-encompassing power and beauty of the universal spirit.

At the same time, you must respect the individuality of others, respect their honesty, respect them. You also must respect nature, the universe, and everything in it. The ant is just as important, and just as majestic, as the redwood; the beauty and wonder of the rising sun is just as marvelous as the miracle of birth and the beautiful perfection of an infant. If you do not have the proper respect for every one of life's miracles—the big and the small—then you have not yet allowed yourself to see fully the wonder of the universe, and you will not be allowed to partake fully of its wonder.

When you have truly adopted these primary virtues of honesty and respect, you will find more virtues naturally springing from them. Compassion and tolerance for others come from our own honesty and respect for ourselves and others. Once we honestly respect the rights of everyone and everything in the universe, we automatically become more tolerant of them and we automatically find ourselves feeling more compassion for them. Knowing that we are all worthy of our place in the universe and that we are all entitled to it, we begin to feel more personally anyone's deprivation. Every imposition on someone else, every denial of someone else's right to peace and tranquillity, every act of intolerance becomes an affront to us personally, no different than if we were its direct target.

Living virtuously also connotes living spiritually. As our awakening spirituality grows in strength with each passing day, we will find ourselves effortlessly guiding our every action with principles of compassion, respect, honesty, and tolerance. These are the same principles set forth in every religion by every religious leader. The more we allow the ancient mysteries to awaken within us, the more we allow ourselves to remember the forgotten memory of our eternal past before this life, the more we become unified with the universal spirit, and the more we will unite with the people around us.

As we do, we will find the powers of our mind opening as well, fueled by our connection with our own inner beings and by our connection to the well of energy that exists as the cosmic consciousness.

With your everyday practice of reminding yourself of the seven keys each morning and reviewing how well you did before going to sleep at night, you will find that all seven of the key principles are intricately intertwined yet separate. They are united yet independent, just as we all will be in the coming golden age.

And you will find that your everyday effort not only reinforces your abilities and opens the way to new opportunities and new powers, but that it also reinforces the energy of the age. Every action—both the positive and the negative—reverberates throughout the universe. The more positive actions you pour into the well, the more the well fills with positive actions, and the more the positive returns to you.

Now, as you go forth and step fully, divinely, and majestically into the New Millennium, remember:

Embrace the divinity within yourself.

Awaken the cosmic Christ in your own heart.

Embrace with infinite love and compassion the darker side of your nature. Face it, know it, and transmute it. Don't repress; don't hide; be whole.

Follow your vision, follow your heart—nobody is an expert in handling your life.

You are the captain of your spaceship.

Be loose; be spontaneous; be different; be yourself.

No matter what the external situation, you are the king or queen of your own universe.

Don't parrot other people's words or ideas, no matter if they call themselves authorities or masters.

Let your individuality shine through you. For better or for worse, you are unique and unrepeatable.

Be proud of who you are.


My words have been like a finger pointing the way. Now on the wings of my God's inspiration fly to the New World.

Good luck on your voyage!

All my love,
Walter

A Spanish-language edition of this book is also
available in paperback

# MAS ALLA DEL HORIZONTE
## Visiones del Nuevo Milenio

por Walter Mercado

at bookstores now!